ART INTO LANDSCAPE

AN EXHIBITION OF SCHEMES TO ENLIVEN PUBLIC SPACES

PRIZE-WINNING AND SELECTED ENTRIES FROM THE SECOND COMPETITION ORGANISED BY THE ARTS COUNCIL OF GREAT BRITAIN IN COLLABORATION WITH THE R I B A, THE LANDSCAPE INSTITUTE AND THE SUNDAY TIMES

16 JULY - 14 AUGUST   SERPENTINE GALLERY LONDON

Arts Council of Great Britain

ISBN 0 7287 0139 1

Preface

The first *Art into Landscape* exhibition in 1974 clearly demonstrated that, when it comes to improving their surroundings, artists, bankers, housewives and children have as much imagination as professional planners and architects. Their ideas for transforming widely differing sites – from vast areas of industrial dereliction to tiny pockets of neglected parkland – were greeted enthusiastically by the critics, the public and even by those responsible for the sites. But no funds were available for realising even the most exciting proposals; none was implemented.

The 1977 exhibition will have more permanent and visible results. The competition has again been open to all, with classes for professionals, amateurs and children, but entrants have had to design projects for one of twelve pre-selected sites chosen by Lord Esher, Mark Boyle, Ian Nairn, David Rock and Tony Southard from the many offered by local authorities all over the country. The same panel chose the 150 entries on show out of more than 1,000 received. The prize-winning schemes were announced on the eve of the exhibition.

After *Art into Landscape* closes, each authority will display locally the alternative proposals for its own site. Thus the people who would actually be affected by them will be able to see the skill, inspiration and sheer range of ideas which competitors have brought to the bleaker spots in some of our cities. Perhaps some will be moved to propose their own ideas for under-used public spaces.

We are immensely grateful to the many local authorities who offered problem areas in their cities, and especially to the ten whose sites were selected. These authorities hope to provide money for the realisation of some of the best schemes (helped by contributions from the Arts Council) and in this way to make appropriately lasting memorials to Silver Jubilee Year.

The difficult tasks of reducing the original list of sites to a manageable number, and of selecting the 150 finalists, were carried out by the jury with great care, good humour and understanding of the practical problems. We owe special thanks to Ian Nairn, who also helped to judge the 1974 competition, which grew out of his enthusiastic response to the late Hubert Dalwood's original inspiration.

In order to avoid a uniformity in presentation, finalists were given as free a hand as possible in the development of their proposals, and the final selection of exhibits was made at the eleventh hour. This further complicated the judges' task and led to some inconsistency between what is in the catalogue and what is on show. We believe this is more than justified by the rich variety of the results.

Once again *Art into Landscape* owes much to the whole-hearted support of the Royal Institute of British Architects, the Landscape Institute and The Sunday Times. We are also grateful to those sponsors whose generosity has allowed us to reward the prize-winning proposals:

IBM United Kingdom Limited
London Weekend Television
The Sunday Times
H J Heinz Company Limited
Sheffield City Council
Courtaulds Limited, Worsted Spinning Division, Spennymoor
Greater London Council
B C A Limited, a member of the Blue Circle Group
The Scottish Arts Council
Coventry Evening Telegraph
Imperial Chemical Industries Limited, Agricultural and Petrochemicals Division
Philips Electronic and Associated Industries Limited
North of England Newspapers

Three of these, I B M United Kingdom Limited, The Sunday Times and the Greater London Council, also supported the first competition.

This unprecedented co-operation between local government, industry, the press and the Arts Council has been heartening – not least to the competitors whose enthusiasm and invention promise much for the future of our environment.

Sue Grayson
Serpentine Gallery Organiser
July 1977

Schemes are arranged in 12 sections according to site. Within each section entries appear in the alphabetical order of competitors' names. Catalogue entry numbers correspond with exhibition numbers.

Proposals were submitted and judged in 4 categories: professional (artists, architects, landscape architects, engineers and students of these professions); laymen; children and school groups. Entrants identified by a number only are in the professional category; lay entrants are marked L; children C and school groups SG.

Brief	Site	Entries
1	Elland Bridge	1– 9
2	North East Ironmasters Area	10–20
3	Open Space at Spon End	21–28
4	Spennymoor Slagheaps	29–37
5	Roundabout at Ware	38–51
6	Kelvingrove Art Gallery and Museum	52–61
7	Finsbury Park, London	62–82
8	Lambeth Walk, London	83–96
9	125 Rotherhithe Street, Southwark, London	97–110
10	Sheffield Wall	111–131
11	Eastbourne, Stockton-on-Tees	132–138
12	Kingsbury Water Park	139–151

The catalogue reflects the fact that professionals and amateurs still use imperial and metric measurements.

Elland Bridge

Riverside revival to restore a Pennine valley panorama

The site is located on the eastern side of the A629 where it crosses the River Calder at Elland Bridge. Elland Bridge is approximately two miles south of Halifax town centre and half a mile north of Elland centre. The site comprises three acres. It is owned by Calderdale Metropolitan Borough Council.

Site Description

The site is an irregularly shaped but level area of land currently overgrown and bestrewn with rubbish. The River Calder, which is heavily polluted, forms the boundary to the north and the southern boundary is marked by a stone setted track. There are clumps of hedgerow trees on the site but none are protected by tree preservation orders. Access to the site is from Millgate.

The site is prominent from the A629 and will be even more so, once the new Elland by-pass, which skirts the eastern and northern boundaries of the site is completed in 1978. The site surrounds are potentially quite dramatic; to the north the valley sides are steep and tree covered, and to the south the prospect of the buildings of Elland covering the hillside presents a cogent urban mass. However the valley bottom itself has been marred by industry. Dereliction and dilapidation are apparent, and the presence of a power station and gasometers to the east of the site combine to describe a depressing picture.

Existing Planning Policies and Constraints

Part of the site is at present being used as a materials compound by the contractor for the Elland by-pass. The road contract will be of two years' duration finishing in 1978, and the site will be vacated on completion of the contract. The existing access to the site at Millgate is an unadopted road, and because of poor sight-lines is unsuitable for heavy volumes of vehicular traffic. An alternative access is possible from Century Road which would be more suitable for heavy vehicular flows; obtaining access from this point would, however require negotiation with private land owners.

The Yorkshire River Authority have a scheme to straighten the River Calder and construct a cascade, which would add some land to the site. Although the scheme has been prepared in detail, progress has been halted through lack of finance and no definite programme has been declared. There is however no reason why the scheme to improve the site should not proceed before the project to straighten the river.

The site is included within the Council's Derelict Land Improvement Scheme. Grant aid from the Department of the Environment was applied for in 1973, before local government re-organisation, by the former Elland U.D.C. and a sum of £7,750 was confirmed. The Department of the Environment has since reaffirmed that this grant is still available with appropriate updating to account for inflation. Calderdale Council's Development Services Committee is being asked to confirm in principle that a financial grant will be available to assist in the realisation of a suitable scheme.

A District Plan is currently being prepared for the area surrounding the site. Although this plan has not yet been formally adopted it recommends large scale recreational usage and general improvement of areas in the valley bottom. The use of the site for recreation would be appropriate.

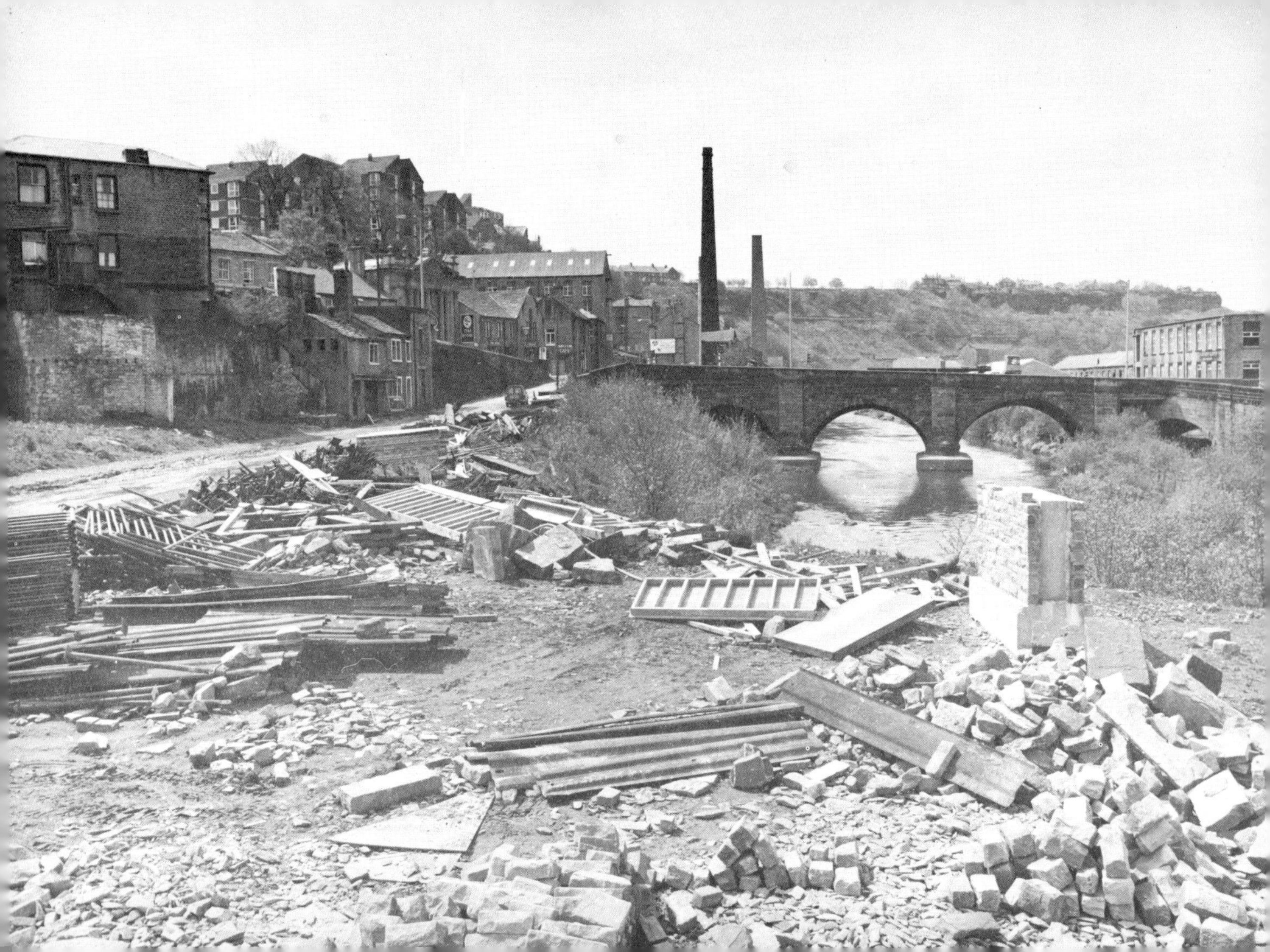

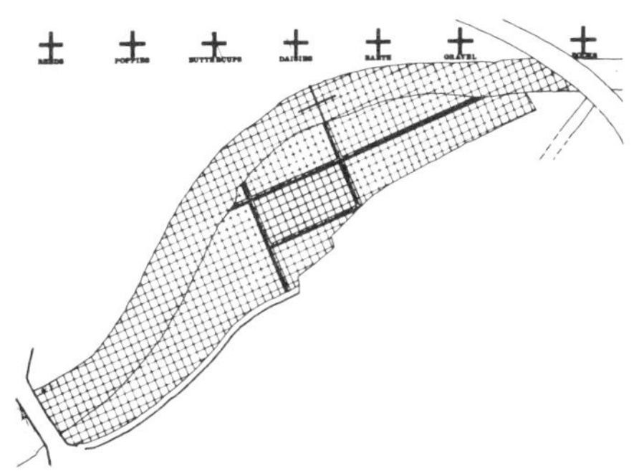

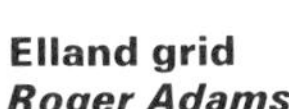

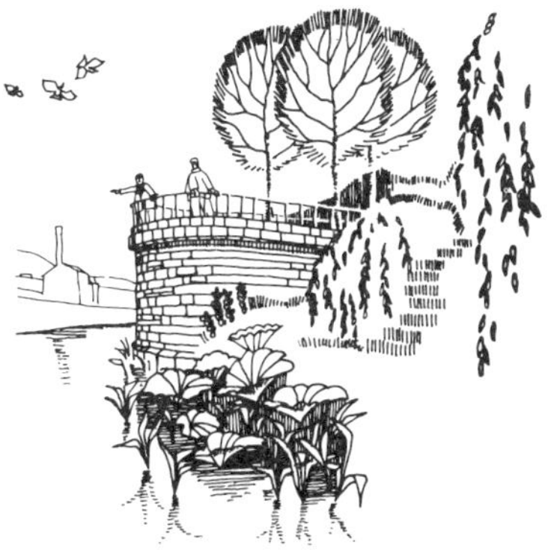

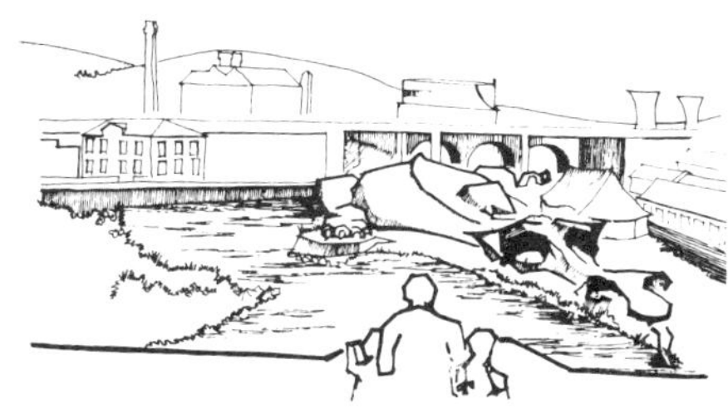

Elland grid
Roger Adams

A five metre grid is imposed on the site. At every intersection on the grid is a $1\frac{1}{2} \times 1\frac{1}{2}$ m cross. The axis of the grid is determined by the position of the two bridges. The proposal incorporates an existing arched pipeline which falls on the grid. Four excavated vistas are aligned with the grid, and these vistas form the perimeter of a lawn which is divided into two squares by a row of cross shaped seats. The lawn which is covered with crosses of white daisies would be of 'bowling green' standard; this will contrast with the remaining wild area. Crosses of reeds run from the bridge and up the banking gradually diminishing into a two dimensional form. Crosses of rocks in the river bed prevent congestion between crosses of reeds. An area of river-bed would be excavated for swimming and a changing platform is formed at the junction of two of the vistas. The relationship between the formal grid and the processes of nature would be interesting to watch.

Born 1954 in Doncaster. Studies interior design at Middlesex Polytechnic.

A riverside park
Mike Baldwin

The site is developed as an open green enclosed by landscaped banks between which a path meanders through a variety of spaces. To the north east end of the green is a 'club house', a simple timber-framed building capable of being built by unskilled volunteers and which uses existing services. Car access is from Century Road and leads to limited parking beneath the trees behind the club house. It is envisaged that in the future river pollution will be reduced and the riverside will become a great asset. Four belvederes of re-used stone overlook the river, and access to the banks is by steps to picnic/fishing areas. The landscape design will be 'semi-wild', thus minimising maintenance and planting on imported topsoil is to be low cost, hardy, pollution-tolerant and fast-growing. A limited number of extra large trees will mark the belvederes. From within the site the gas-works, by-pass and blank brick factory extension on Century Road are screened by poplars.

Born 1949 in Hyde, Cheshire. Studied at Sheffield University. Works as architect.

Dragon
Nicholas Cook

In the mill town of Elland lives a dragon who sips the cool river Calder and wallows, half submerged, having crawled from the moors to rest amongst the people of Elland. His head protrudes, neck in a pool and body rising majestically, offsetting the scale of the new by-pass. Alone he wallows, the friend of all, providing a sanctuary for the elderly, and a place for folk to sit and admire the views, flowers, shrubs and trees which abound on his exciting torso. Space is allocated for a future marquee, clubhouse, day centre or stage. Individual features, head, limbs and parts of the tail are constructed of demolition and waste material already on site, collected or even donated. Items of historical and local interest, foundation stones, lamps, railings and other decorative features are integrated in the dragon. The body is of excavated earth from local slagheaps, planted with broad leaf and evergreen trees; pool and lawns complete the wonder of the Elland dragon.

Born 1954 in Leeds. Studies at Oxford School of Architecture.

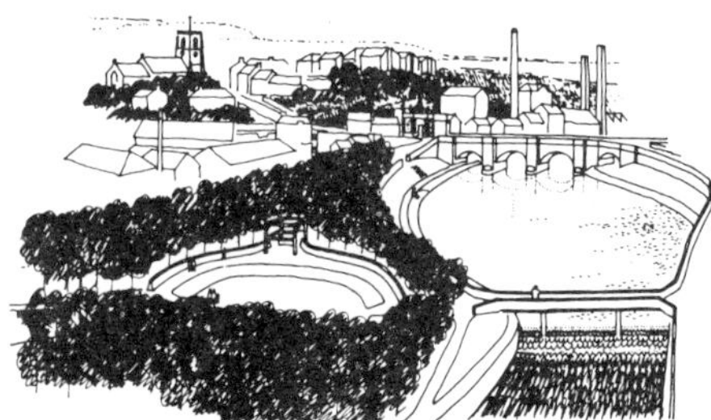

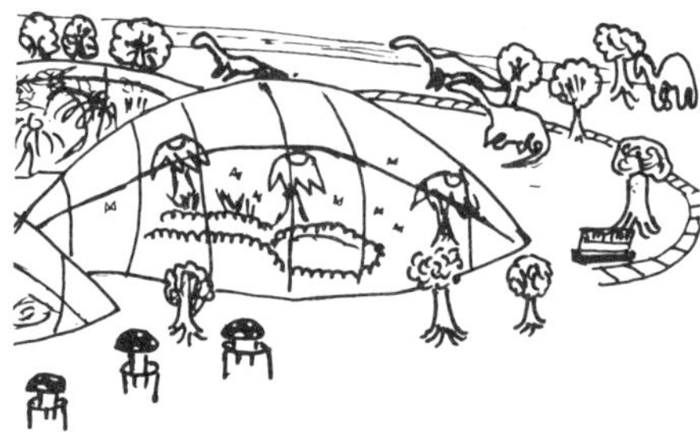

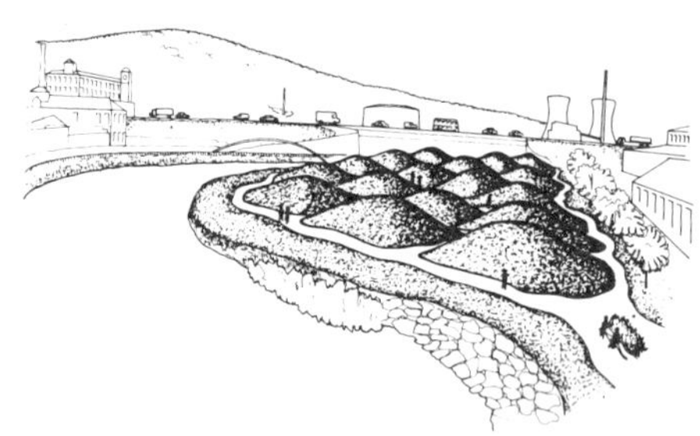

The Ballad of Elland Feud
David Ellis

Elland means 'land by the river', which describes the site itself. The Church, Hall and Mill were all equidistant from the Bridge and each other, and there is a connection through the verses of a medieval ballad which tells of the feud between Eland of Eland, High Sheriff of Yorkshire, and his neighbours. The climax is on Palm Sunday 1351 when the last of the Elands are slain crossing the river from the Hall to Church by their adversaries who had hidden in the Mill overnight. My design draws the threads together again, with trees, still waters, reflections and quiet walks. On the site of the Mill is a space for people to gather, approached along a channel of stones from the weir and entered through the re-erected medieval frame of the Hall. Around the space is a low wall carrying in relief the 118 verses of the Ballad.

Born 1940 in Marsden, Yorkshire. Studied at the Huddersfield School of Architecture, and Leeds School of Town Planning. Teaches at Manchester Polytechnic School of Architecture.

Kubla Khan's Kingdom
Jeremy Franks, Simon Laye

At Elland Bridge did Sunday Times
Some stately pleasure domes decree,
Where Calder, murky river, ran
Through factories measureless to man
Down to a sunless sea.
So half a mile of barren ground
With paths and rails was girdled round
And there were gardens bright, which flowers filled,
Where blossomed toadstools, selling tea,
And here were monsters ancient as the hills,
To guard the sunny spots of greenery.
(With apologies to Coleridge and a little help from our friends.)

Like Kubla Khan, we thought we'd build pleasure domes, only ours would be made of transparent plastic with tropical plants, butterflies and tropical fish pool, heated by solar energy. Outside there is a small-gauge railway running round the site, weaving in between trees and giant fibreglass dinosaurs.

Jeremy Franks and Simon Laye both born 1968 and attend Gledhow Primary School, Leeds.

Riverside mounds
Henry Skrzypecki

The proposal is for a sculptural landscape consisting of grass mounds and meandering paths. Travellers along the adjacent by-pass and railway would view these as rhythmic forms contrasting with the surrounding urban mass. The landscape, as well as being a visual event, is intended to be a place where visitors can relax or stroll along the riverbank between grass mounds into articulated secluded spaces. The mounds aid the screening of the dereliction and dilapidation apparent in the valley from the visitor, whilst allowing views of upper tree-covered valley slopes. During hours of sunset the longer shadows cast would visually enhance the mound shapes and the visitor would have the added experience of walking into and out of sunlit areas. When occasional minor river flooding or misting occurs the grass mounds would be transformed into riverside islands.

Born 1949 in Halifax. Studied at Huddersfield Polytechnic School of Architecture. Works as architect.

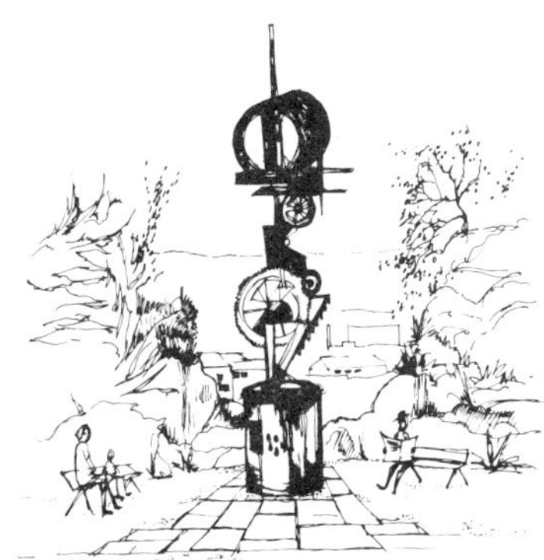

Iron park
Carol Smith

Because of the inaccessibility of this site a scheme here must have visual impact and stimulate interest from a distance. My proposal involves the creating of sculptural forms up to a height of 20 ft constructed of scrap machinery from local industries. These sculptures will be placed within a framework of structure planting including such vigorous trees as willow, poplar and alder. I envisage the park being used by 'lunchtime' workers from surrounding factories hence the informal seating around the two main sculptures. Because reclaimed materials will be used the cost will be low, the only major expenditure being on soft landscape treatment and labour. I also envisage a low maintenance policy.

Born 1956 in Huddersfield. Studied landscape architecture for one year. Now taking one year foundation course at Batley Art College.

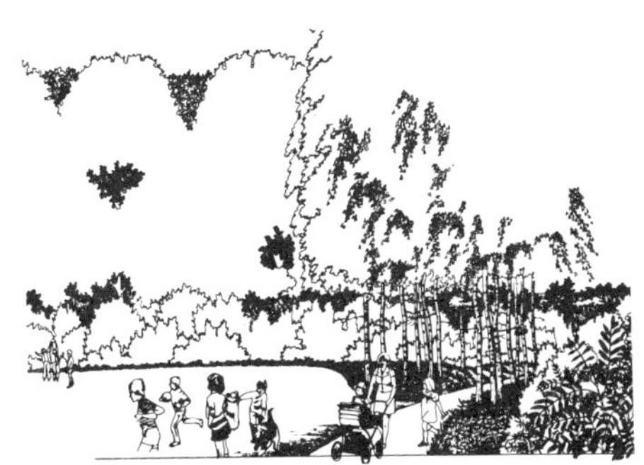

Return to nature
Robert Stokes

The objective is to transform this untidy parcel of industrial fringe into a natural-looking semi-wild landscape of meadows, thicket and woodland and make it available for recreational use. Maintenance could be minimal. Long summer grasses swaying with wild flowers is the most beautiful of all close-up landscapes, growing as free and colourful as an old-fashioned meadow. This necessitates only occasional cutting, once or twice a year in non-intensively used areas. Thicket and woodland require little attention, other than occasional thinning and clearing. Indigenous trees and shrubs, individually providing visual interest with their flowers and fruit, produce a naturally homogeneous enclosure of vigorous and lush foliage; and woodland can be underplanted with drifts of bluebells, ferns and other woodland plants.

Born 1949 in Hastings. Studies at Canterbury College of Art School of Architecture.

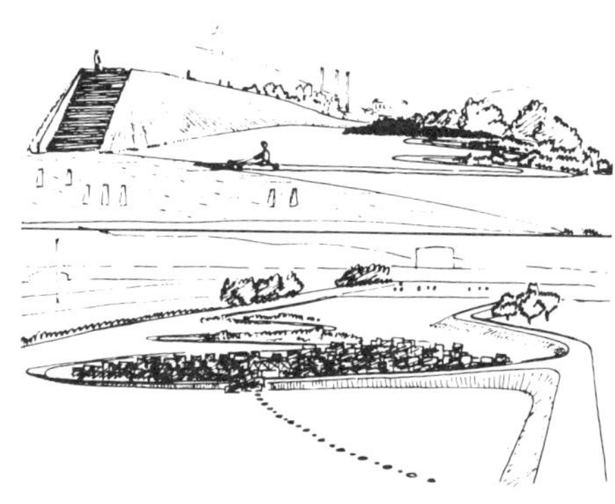

Bogie slope – maze castle
Roger Watkins

Because the immediate surroundings of the Elland Bridge site are rather grey and depressing I thought it would be difficult to revive the site and draw people to it unless it catered for some kind of activity. I got the idea for a bogie slope when I happened to be warning my own children not to take their bogie beyond the end of our street because of the traffic danger. When designing the slope I kept this warning in the front of my mind and I tried to make the slope and the site as safe as possible while at the same time providing a long, exciting and varied run that children could not find elsewhere. Other features in the design, the maze castle and roller skaters' area are included for visual variety and provide other activities for when children tire of playing on the slope itself.

Born 1939 in Manchester. Studied English language and literature at St John's College, Oxford. Works as English teacher—at present unemployed.

Cleveland County Council and
Middlesbrough Borough Council

North East Ironmasters Area

The tide is turning on the Tees – help turn the tide!

The River Tees flows through the heart of Cleveland, almost unnoticed and unused by most people except industry. This is a pity since the Tees could become an attractive feature, offering a wide range of opportunities for recreation and leisure, as well as for industry and shipping.

However, the North East Ironmasters is one piece of land by the River Tees which is to be redeveloped by Middlesbrough Borough Council for riverside recreational purposes as well as for light industry. The North East Ironmasters is located on the south bank, and within the loop of the River Tees, about a mile north west of Middlesbrough Town Centre. Middlesbrough Town Centre is regarded as the main shopping and office centre for the whole of Cleveland country.

The competition site is part of the original ironworks founded in Middlesbrough in the mid-19th century. The Ironmasters district at one time comprised eleven ironworks and rolling mills which produced one third of Britain's pig-iron output. The site has remained virtually unused and derelict for some time, following the movement downstream of the new "land hungry" iron and steel works towards the Tees estuary. The site is a challenging one. The provision of the riverside landscaped walkway and recreation area is seen as an integral part of the redevelopment of the North East Ironmasters, both in terms of bringing people back to the river and also as part of providing an attractive environment for the industrial development.

Brief

Entries are invited for the "face-lifting" of a strip of land by the riverside (1,100 metres long) as a landscaped walkway. The landscaped walkway is to be a prominent part of the proposed long distance walkway along an 8-mile stretch of the River Tees. At one point along the Ironmasters walkway a slag mound has been retained to form the basis of a major viewing point of riverside activities. The mound is a unique feature on the otherwise flat valley of the River Tees; commanding fine views of the shipyard on the opposite bank, the Transporter Bridge and Middlesbrough Docks downstream of the site, and of the Regional Centre and the Cleveland Hills beyond.

Seating and other amenities in the vicinity of the mound would benefit visitors to the area as well as people employed within the industrial estate. There is scope for the development of an area which may be used for ball games on an informal basis on land adjoining the mound.

The River Tees is a tidal river and is grossly polluted. However it is intended to gradually improve the quality of the river in the foreseeable future. Any treatment of the banks will have to take these factors into account.

There is little soil on site. If substantial "soft" landscaping is envisaged sufficient quantities of top and sub soil will have to be improved. Landscaping over a high voltage electricity cable will be restricted and no mounding or tree planting should occur within the cable track or in any positions where tree roots may interfere with the cables. The Acklam Fabrication Works of the British Steel Corporation will remain on the site. The width of the landscaped walkway will be retricted therefore, to less than the average width (22 metres) in the vicinity of the works.

The walkway should not only be suitable for pedestrians but also cyclists and for any maintenance vehicles that may be necessary. Barriers along the edge of the river bank are necessary to maximise safety of the walkway users. At some points along the river industrial concerns may require occasional access to the river for import/export purposes. Therefore, any proposals should allow for the periodic temporary closure of the walkway to allow the safe and convenient access to the river for firms. A public car parking area adjacent to the River Tees is proposed. The proposed road immediately south of the mounded area provides the only other means of public vehicular access to the riverside in this area and a small amount of space for public car parking may be appropriate in this area too.

Climate

The River Tees lies within the coldest and driest half of the British Isles. Temperatures average about 9 degrees centigrade over the year. Dominant winds are from the south and west. These winds are also the strongest, especially in autumn and winter. Winds from the north and north-east are characteristically gentle but cold.

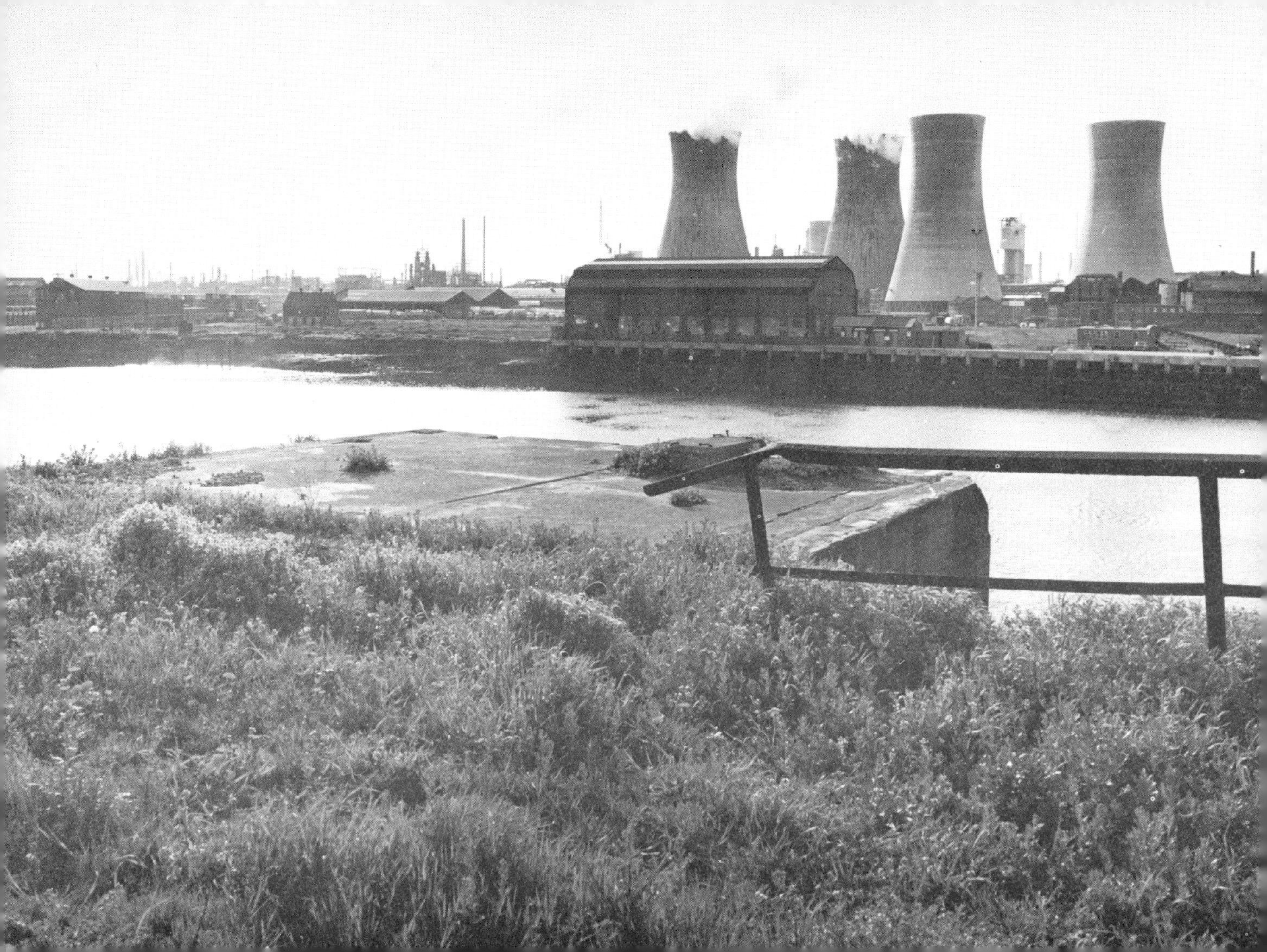

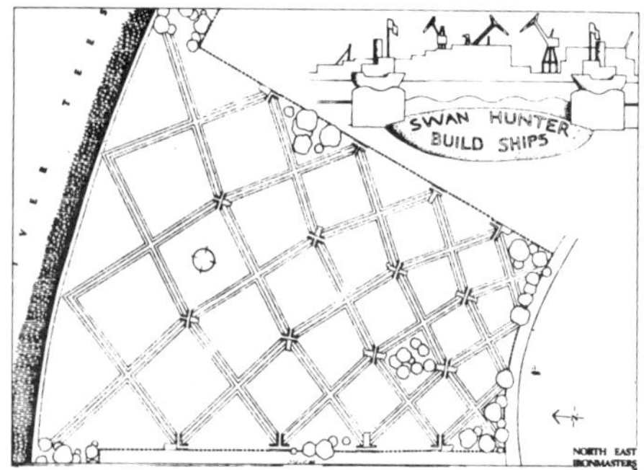

Promenade and factory gardens
Ed Bowness

I suggest that firms on the industrial estate maintain the part of the walkway adjacent to their premises. Each firm would also be allocated a plot defined by the grid that dissects an area of council land adjoining the riverside path. This grid, expressed by footpaths and hedges, is contructed in such a way as to provide four-sided enclosures, increasing in size towards the river. Larger firms will be responsible for larger plots nearer the river. Competition will be encouraged by an annual prize awarded to the best plot and by the possibility of considerable local prestige. Unallocated plots will be available as public recreation ground. The grid includes a sizeable mound on which will be sited a telescope station offering views of the river activities . . . docks, shipyards and the transporter bridge. The grid would contain a delightful array of public and semi-public spaces connected by iron gates leading to topiary bridges.

Born 1954 in Wiltshire. Studies environmental design at Middlesex Polytechnic

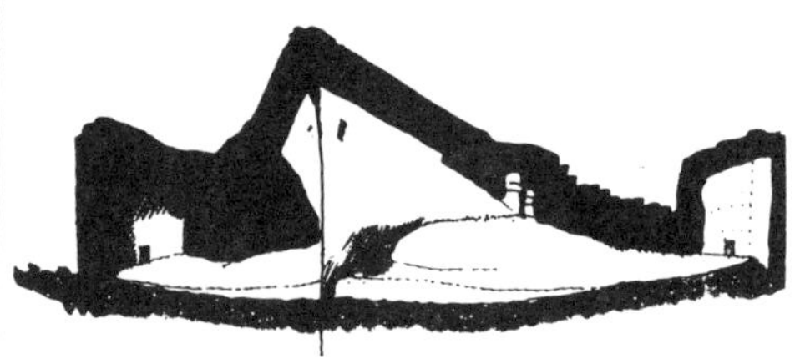

A monument to shipbuilding
Thomas Brent

In attempting to create an industrial promenade I have been influenced by the superfluous scrap metal in an area of shipbuilding. A contrast is struck between the occasional developing vessel across the river and the decrepit hull on the mound, seen as a focal point. The walk is envisaged as being tranquil with the hull as a monument to which respect is paid, the diminishing doorways of the steel barriers accelerating this aided at the outset by a darkening blanket of poppies growing through the gridded clinker path, gradually blending into the softening lush grasses culminating at the mound. Hence each bay becomes calmer and more secluded by the increasing height of the barriers. On arrival at the mound the visitor would be daunted by the planted section of hull yet from the grassy deck the core of the British shipbuilding industry can be seen. The monument therefore has a recreational and spiritual value.

Born 1950 in London. Studies interior design at Middlesex Polytechnic.

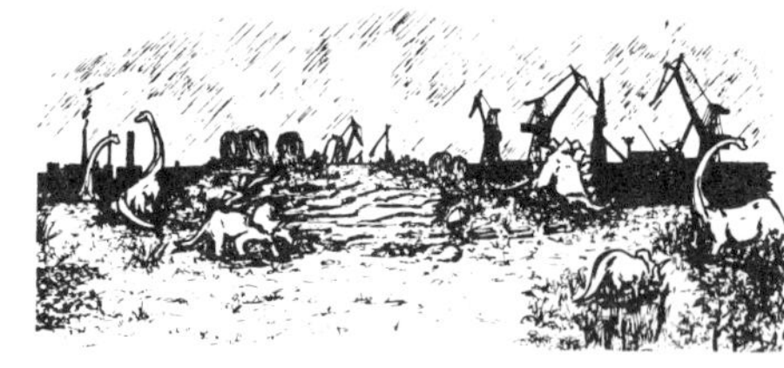

Teessaurus playground
Geneviève Glatt

The site needs life — forms sympathetic to the environment but large and powerful enough to compete with surrounding structures. Monsters . . .? Dinosaurs came to mind. They roam freely around the mound, which is kept open with low vegetation as a viewing platform overlooking the Tees and shipyards. A terraced south slope offers a good standpoint over the 'field' provided for various activities (ballgames, meetings etc). Concrete picnic tables shelter from the north wind, behind Stegasaurus — children can slide down the slope to ride on Triceratops before going up again in Brontosaurus' footsteps. The whole area is envisaged as a 'little piece of countryside' where each plant has a contribution to make. This scheme could provide a refreshing place in the hard, down-to-earth world in which it stands.

Born 1936 in France. Trained as nurse. Now studies interior design at Teesside Polytechnic.

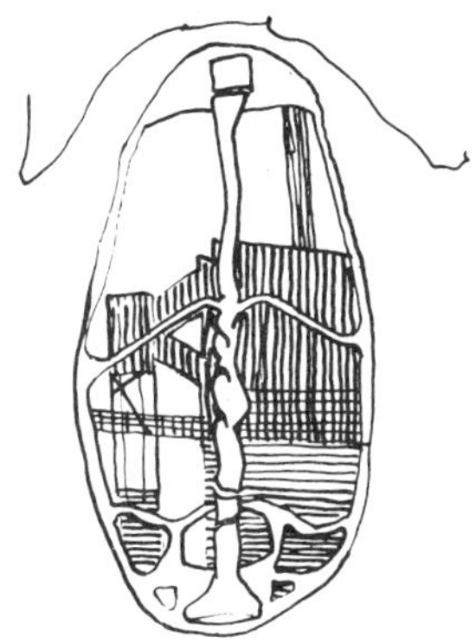

Wall of change with antique windows
Rosemary Ind

A strip of waste land beside a polluted windswept river. Stripped of its history, this has become no-place. A wall is proposed, with a path on both sides. The wall is crinkle-crankle to provide calm zones, with breaks in its length, to allow the walker to change sides when the wind changes. Because the industrial view is good—cranes, cooling towers, a transporter bridge—and to provide a past, antique windows are set into the wall. Windows presuppose looking. The no-place looked at through the windows of the past acquires a present, and from its present the future.

'Time present and time past
Are both perhaps present in time future,
And time future contained in time past.'
T S Eliot *Burnt Norton.*

Born in India. Studied at the Architectural Association. Works as architect/free-lance designer.

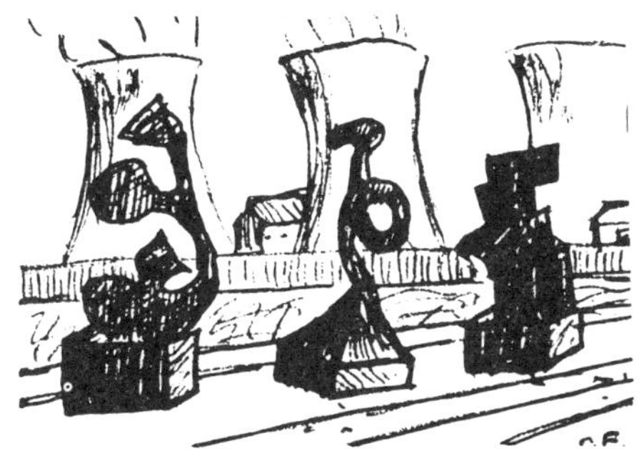

Riverside re-creation
The Laurence Jackson School, Guisborough, Cleveland.

Our proposals are to produce a better place to relax in, a better place to look at, and a better place to look from. We suggest both cycle and walking tracks on the river bank, seats strategically placed for older people and a ball-playing area which would be a boon to workers and to older children. Plants already growing should be encouraged to grow more abundantly. We would collect the bricks, slag, driftwood and scrap wood strewn in the area for re-use on the wharf, which would be an ideal place for 3-D display; the sides of buildings could be decorated with relief work. Schools, the local Art College and local artists could all make a contribution by using local materials. The mound is our viewing-point and places of interest both distant and near are indicated on the flat top of the summit's shelter wall.

Form 3R (3rd year form ages 13 to 14 years).

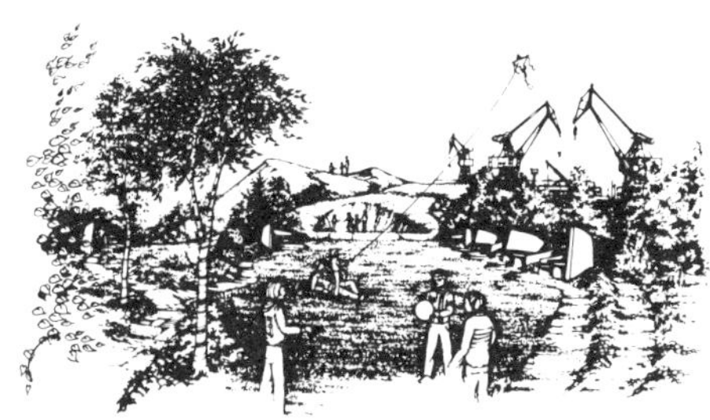

Ironstone wynde
George Middlemiss

For visual and practical reasons large areas of the existing boulder slag surface is retained, and prevailing local weather conditions and other practical factors influence the layout and juxtaposition of activity and non-activity areas, their boundaries being defined by the strategic positioning of clump planting, climatic shelters and meandering pedestrian ways. The riverside way is separated naturally from the group activity areas by the mound which becomes a viewing platform, stage, backcloth and focal point to the natural amphitheatre defined by a landscape layout which creates an illusion of seclusion without restricting the freedom of public movement or vision. Additionally, this produces changing views stimulated by the interplay between surrounding industrial scenes and surface patterns through which the pedestrian walkways wind.

Born 1945. Studied at Newcastle College of Art. Lectures on furniture/interior design at Teesside Polytechnic.

14SG

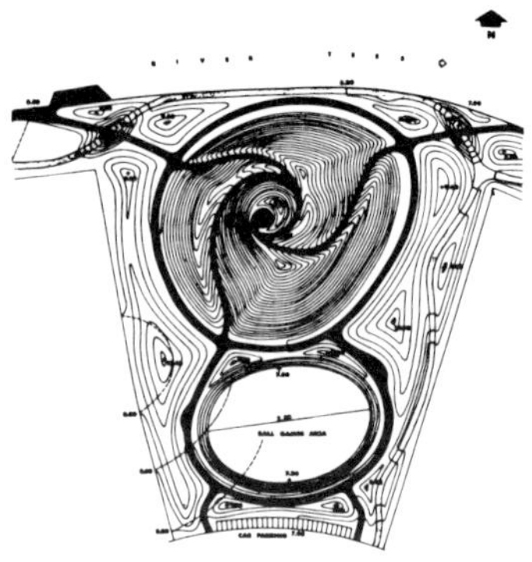

Jubilee Hill
Mary Mitchell

The iron works at Middlesbrough that once provided one third of Britain's pig iron have been closed and this site will provide land for light industry, warehousing and landscaping. I propose that the open space be remodelled to give character to a dominant sculptured mound known as Jubilee Hill, protection to the sunken ball games area and a feeling of enclosure, interest and variety whilst walking through the bold formations from the car park to the riverside. Paths form an integral part of the overall layout: they are incorporated in the landscape and lead to the top of Jubilee Hill along the river, connect with sitting areas and form a link with the new factories. The cycleway leads from the distributor road to the riverside area. Overall tree planting provides interest, shelter and a screen against industry. Owing to the simplicity of the project maintenance is minimal.

Born 1923 in Downton. Studied horticulture and landscape architecture. Works as landscape architect.

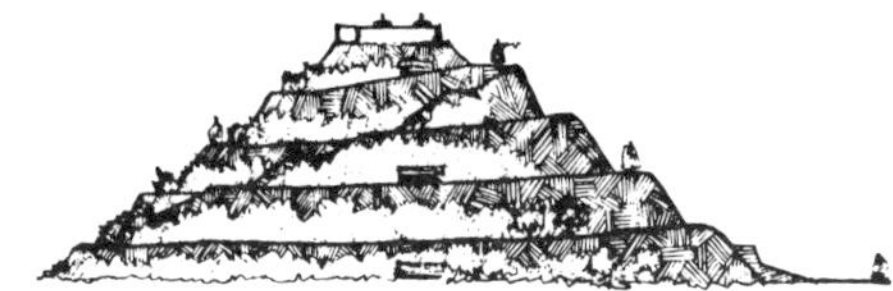

Meandering round the bend
Keith Robinson

The aim is to make the pedestrian conscious of being in touch with the river, without being forced into the rigid concept of the 'towpath', by deliberately taking routes away from, then back to, the river edge, and providing constantly changing views. There are two distinct movement systems – formal and informal. The formal route is suitable for pedestrians and wheeled traffic, but the informal route is rougher and only suitable for pedestrians. Both routes meander through the site, the informal route undulating as well. It is proposed to form mounds as focal points for items of local industrial archeology. The river bank is opened up at intervals to permit closer appreciation of the river and to allow occasional vehicular access to revitalise wharf facilities. Vehicles are necessary intruders – their presence could contribute positively to the riverside scene and help inject new life into this bank of the Tees.

Born 1946 in Bredbury. Studied architecture at Nottingham University. Works as architect.

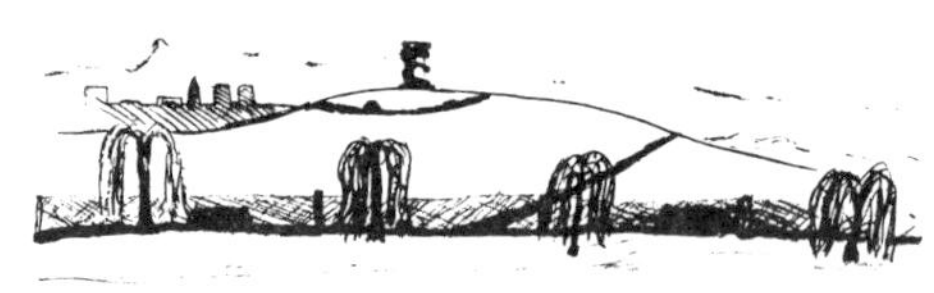

Turning the tide
St Michael's School, Middlesbrough

The aim of this plan is to provide an attractive but not too ambitious scheme with the emphasis on its function as an area for leisure and recreation to cater for all ages. At present the site is unsafe, being open to the river along its edge and in parts treacherous underfoot. The target cost of the scheme imposes limits; so this is a simple plan which would give this part of the riverside an attractive face-lift. The main elements of the plan are: a riverside walkway fenced from the river bank and edges by grass and willow trees; a riverside quay; car parking facilities; play area; information centre and landscaped mound with viewpoint.
'The tide must turn, the time has come –
A revolution of new ideas.
The generation of today has decided
To change the town . . .' (K Groves)

Christine Chapman, Karen Groves, Peter Henry, Gavin Parry, Karina Thompson, aged 14–15 years. All attend St Michael's R.C. Comprehensive School, Middlesbrough.

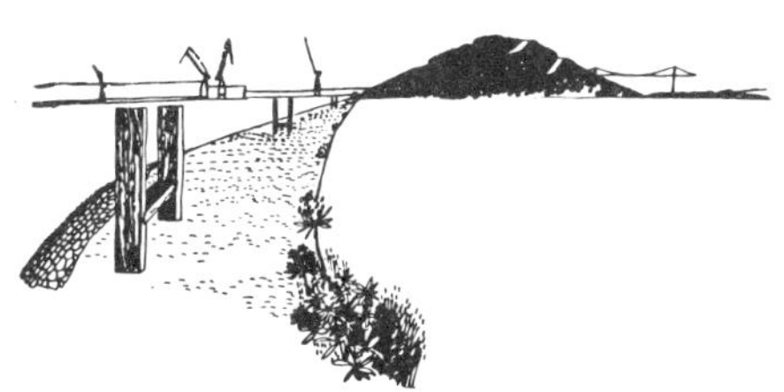

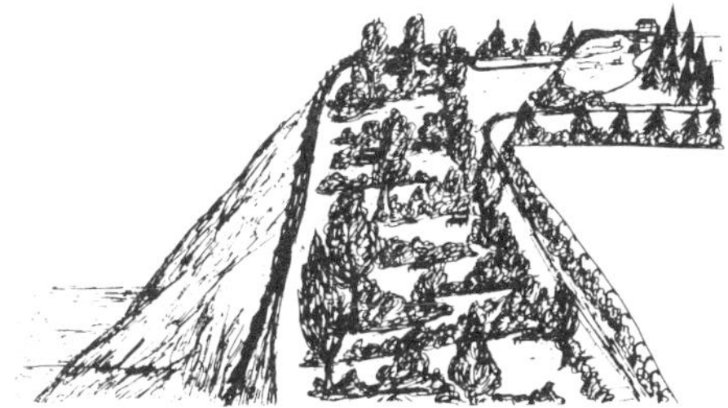

Tees pudding
Peter Smithson

The site is on a really striking bend in the river . . . an idea! point for signalling that the river is beginning to live again. There is already a low mound on the water's edge. My proposal is to make it dramatically higher, so it becomes as steep and as intriguing as Castle Hill at nearby Bishopton, and to plant it all over with gorse. As gorse flowers all year round this pudding-shaped yellow mound will be the signal. To provide fun, two paths will spiral up the mound to a viewing circle on its summit. From here the industrial wonders of Teesside, as well as Roseberry Topping and Captain Cook's Monument, should be clearly visible. Along the river walk I would prefer to put barriers only at danger points. The path itself would be gravel-surfaced hoggin only, with topsoil spread on either side. This new soil would be encouraged to self-seed after some initial years of schoolchildren collecting and scattering wild flower seeds.

Born 1923 in Stockton-on-Tees. Works as architect in private practice.

Jubilee riverside gardens
Ivy Watts

This walkway is characterised by a continous line of greenery and a seasonal display of colourful flowering trees, bushes, shrubs and perennial ground covering plants. Two hardsurfaced pathways are provided, one for pedestrians, hugging the riverbank, the other adjacent to the industrial boundary is for cyclists. In wider stretches the pathways will be separated by continous stretches of grass interspersed with clumps of trees and shrubs; the industrial boundary will be screened by prickly bushes. Rose of Sharon and other ground covering plants will spread down the riverbank. The mound will be grassed, its river front covered with heathers. The seating here will overlook the river in all directions, and be adjacent to a tearoom and lavatories, screened at the back by pine trees so as not to break the skyline. Seating will also overlook the play area, itself grassed and screened on three sides by trees and prickly bushes along the industrial boundary and the road.

Born 1930 in Esholt, Yorkshire. Housewife.

Open space at Spon End

The re-use of a small area of land left over from redevelopment. The brief asks for the provision of play facilities for local children and the improvement of the environment of the area by attractive landscaping

A derelict 0.6 acre area of land situated alongside a major footpath route to the city centre which lies about $\frac{1}{2}$ mile to the west. Bounded to the north by the recently pedestrianised Upper Spon Street, the area is overlooked from three sides by residential development (City Council and Housing Association) and open to Windsor Street on the fourth. Being part of a redevelopment area, there is little or no topsoil on site suitable for landscaping purposes. The remains of demolished buildings (floors, footings, etc) are present at or near existing ground level.

Design Brief
1. The provision for childrens play and the availability of open space suitable for such use is very limited in the neighbouring housing areas. It is considered important therefore that this site should be developed primarily to make good this deficiency. The play facilities proposed should be visually acceptable to residents in overlooking property, easily maintained (no water or sand) and resistant to vandalism.
2. New footpaths across the site are required to link the 4-story maisonette development more directly to the main pedestrian route. These should also relate to the siting and disposition of the proposed play facilities. Existing pedestrian circulation around Meadow House needs re-examining in the light of present and future need.
3. It is considered appropriate that soft landscaping — trees, shrubs, grass, ground modelling — should be used to provide the unifying element between this site and its neighbours; particularly careful treatment is needed along the boundary with the pedestrianisation scheme.

The basic plant material specified for the scheme should be tough, vigorous and in keeping with that used elsewhere in the locality.

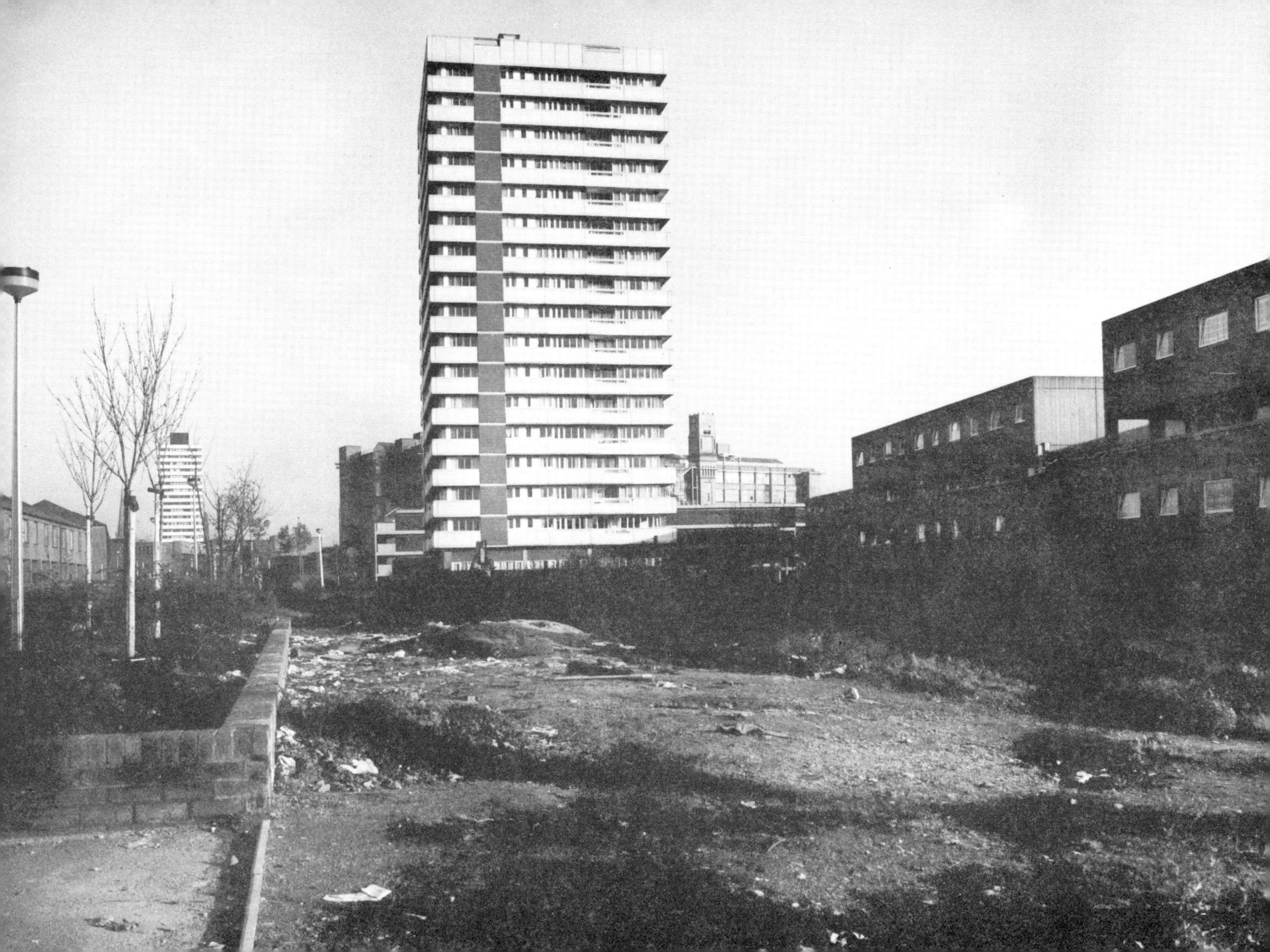

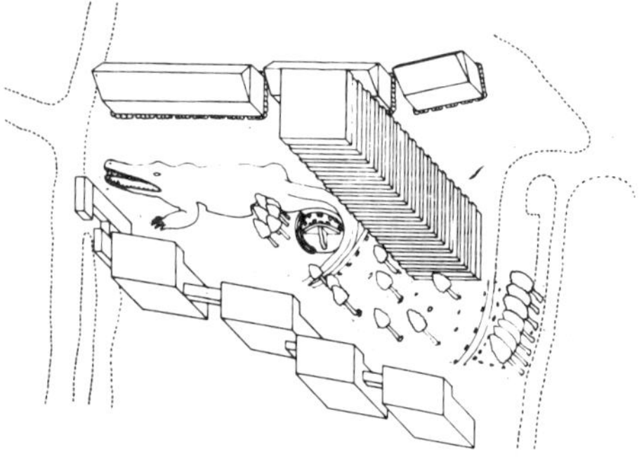

Crocodile
Sue Bowness

I want to create exciting and delightful spaces for the young and old. This incorporates soft landscaping with grass, trees, and flowers; an open air theatre/bandstand with seating for the elderly and pedestrians; an area for the under-fives and an 'adventure crocodile'. The crocodile creates interesting and imaginative spaces of its own. Into the nose is built a long slide, and the full length of its back and tail can be used for cycling and skating up and down. Inside the body, there is enough room for children to build their own play area. Apart from daylight coming through the mouth and entrances, the interior could be lit artificially. Ideally the crocodile and surrounding pathways, seating and theatre/bandstand would be made from granite setts. If this proves too expensive old bricks could be used.

Born 1952 in London. Studies interior design at Middlesex Polytechnic.

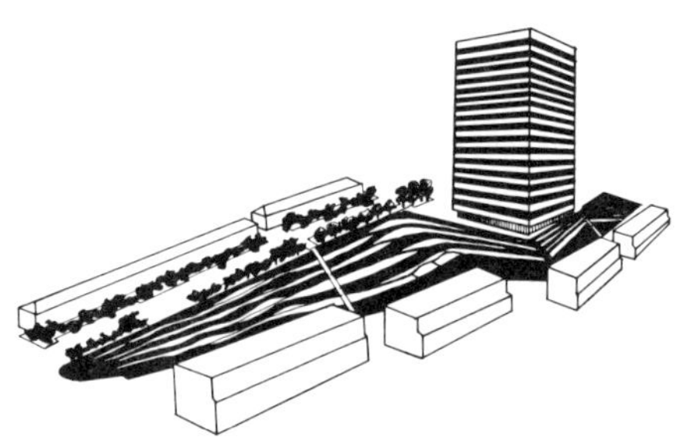

Multi-channelled play
Joan Garretty

Play facilities on housing estates have become limited to uniform concrete shapes and tubular steel, lacking any elements of danger or curiosity. My intention is to revive excitement by means of colour, texture and shape. My proposal is to develop this strip of land into a series of grass-covered hillocks and mounds dissected by four channels varying in length, width and depth. Each channel uses different materials, colours, textures and ideas for play. At ground level there would be some evidence of playgrounds: – noise and occasional glimpses of children – but the real view would be from the estate balconies, allowing mothers to watch their children playing below. People don't want to feel that they are living in a playground, but they don't want a view of unsightly barriers either. A solution is to make the ground itself the visual barrier whilst also making it a part of the playground.

Born 1954 in London. Studies interior design at Middlesex Polytechnic.

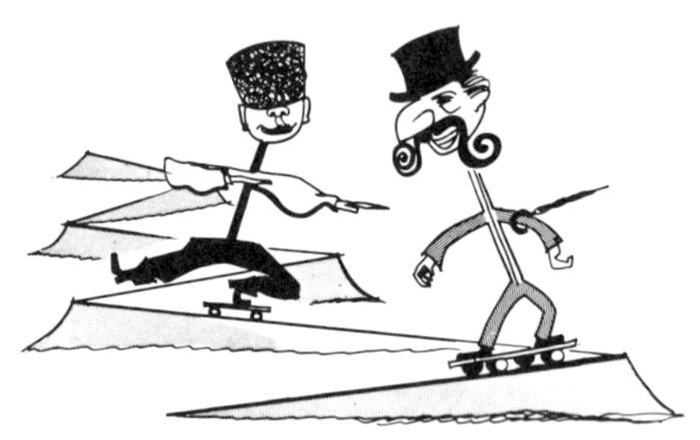

Cresta run
Kenneth Langlois

A 'cresta run' for the safe use of skateboards and soap box chariots is suggested. The natural slopes of the site would be used to the best advantage in laying a fast, true, smooth surface and banked bends will assist cornering. Sandpits beyond will cushion those who overshoot. In the winter the track could be flooded and frozen for skaters. There would be a toddlers' play area featuring a dished area for ball games where the ball-always-comes-back. Sheltered seating for Mums would be a meeting place where shy newcomers to the neighbourhood could make contact. Stabilised with spread gravel, a camp-fire locale enclosed in interlocking steel shuttering would be the neighbourhood barbecue centre and sound-baffled sing-song zone. The entire site would be soft landscaped with hardy shrubs and trees to present the visual, olfactory, aural and tactile senses with changing experiences.

Born 1931 in London. Trained RIBA Library. Works as architect.

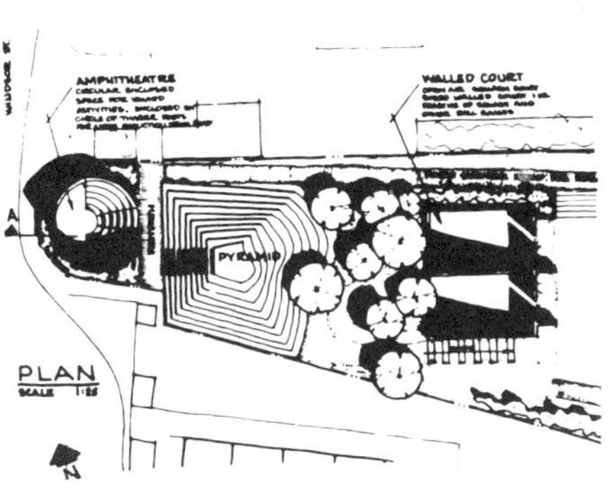

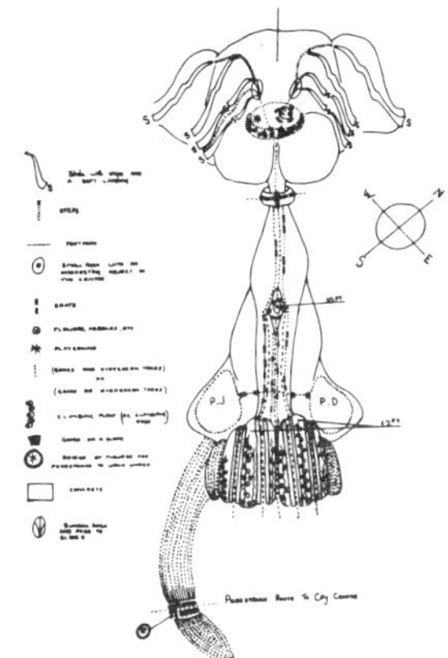

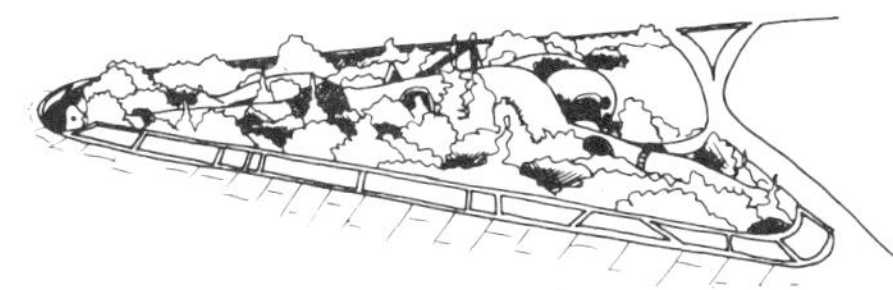

Adventure hollow
Floyd Parks

The greater part of the area has been excavated to produce differences in levels naturally missing from the site. The purpose in this is to allow scope for more varied activities, to help direct noise upwards, reducing the nuisance to surrounding properties and to reduce the direct view of the area by the casual passer-by. This is further strengthened by the placement of trees and shrubbery around the perimeter. The strong definition of the site thus achieved determines an area which children can identify as their own territory. The elements which make up the scheme, i.e. pyramid, ramp, maze, etc. are intended to encourage imaginative, flexible and varied use. These elements can be used by any age-group. However, the scheme does include a special area for small children accompanied by mothers.

Born 1946 in Illinois, USA. Studied at University of Illinois School of Architecture. Works as architect.

Hot dog
Jennifer Ramsay

I wanted to design something that the people could enjoy and which would be an attractive feature of their district. I'd like to think that the local people could supply and plant the flowers, and possibly the local schoolchildren could take an interest in looking after them; and I hope that everyone will have a lot of fun with it. The dog will be built of concrete using plenty of flowers, evergreen trees and shrubs to decorate it. One end (the head) will be used mainly as a playground area with slides running down the sides of the face. There will be footpaths leading down the centre of the dog, joining the main footpath to the city centre. Also for people who don't want to go onto the dog, they can cut through his tail by a footpath which will be surrounded by grass and flowers, etc.

Born 1962. Attends St Bede's School, Reigate, Surrey.

Spon end man
Richard Sharland

The idea is to create a 'secret' play area for smaller children in the midst of an alien urban environment; a place where their activities will be partially hidden from adult scrutiny but which is close enough to their homes for maximum availability and safety. An interesting space for the young imagination, but which keeps a low profile from street level so as to blend with the design of its immediate surroundings and simultaneously break up that design with an island of curves of growth. The proposal is twofold: 1. a hollow sculpture of a prone human being, whose pose suggests several centuries of slumber; once vegetation is well advanced, the figure will be almost completely concealed in a trough surrounded by foliage, which in turn will be enclosed by a concrete rampart decorated with mosaics executed by local school groups. 2. a miniature ampitheatre, truncated by a high painted wall for the playing of ball games, which the windows of the surrounding urban complex forbid.

Born 1952 in London. 'Self employed artist'.

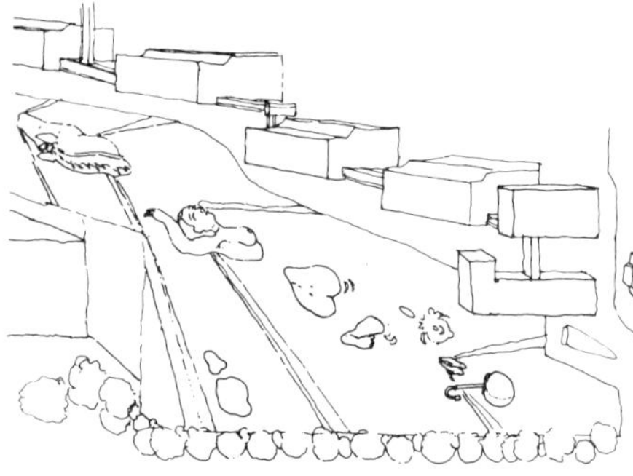

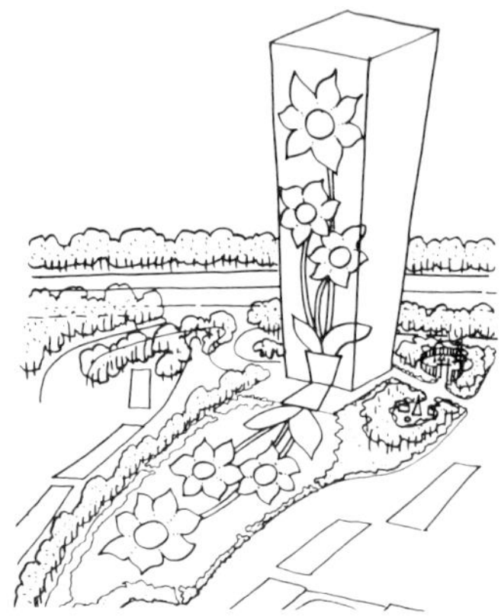

Lady Godiva crosses the Rubicon
David Walker

This is a play sculpture. The surface of the ground is treated as if it is a river. Large-scale figures appear to be swimming across the open space. These figures are made of in situ concrete with a polished finish. They incorporate swings, roundabouts, sand pits, helter skelters and other traditional play structures—modified according to the nature of the figures. The ripples on the surface of the ground are formed by steps, terraces and footpaths. They are so constructed to take advantage of the slope of the site and the sun. The horse's head may be hollow but would only permit supervised access on special occasions. Otherwise maintenance and play equipment can be stored there. A small amount of planting would symbolise splashes and spray at appropriate points.

Born 1940 in Tredegar, South Wales. Studied at RWA School of Architecture, Bristol and University of Bristol. Teaches architecture at Gloucestershire College of Art and Design.

Say it with flowers
Denis R Wilkinson

The idea is to create a giant set of flowers for all the folk locked in the 17 storey tower to look down on. A magnification of the flower-pot of spring bulbs in every window. A flower set in a concrete jungle. The live, growing flower is reflected in the mural facade flower — 17 storeys high, like a mirror from the ground — a giant flower, a perennial for all the community around to see. So you get the flower in nature, bulbs set in grass: snowdrops, scillas, crocuses, daffodils, narcissi and tulips. The different flowering times would give a changing colour flower from January to late May like a changing mirage. Then early in summer the whole thing is mown and reverts to grass for play and such-like. Next year up comes the giant flower again, this time more beautiful than ever. The tower flower becomes an identity symbol turning an ordinary tower (hundreds like 'em all over the country) into a unique tower.

Born in Sunderland. Studied at the University of Durham and University of Pennsylvania. Works as landscape architect.

Sporting chance for Spennymoor Slagheaps

An opportunity to shape the new face of a tired landscape by changing 19th century dereliction to 20th century recreation

The site is situated in central Durham on the south side of road A6074, the Spennymoor Western Link, which skirts the southern edge of the town centre.

Description

The land was formerly used as an ironworks slag tip covering 8 acres of land adjacent to an expanding sports complex which is being developed by Sedgefield District Council. Due to the nature of the tipped material, vegetation is sparse and occurs only around the fringes of the site. The remainder is covered by heaps of bare slag and other debris which presents one of the worst examples of industrial dereliction still left in central Durham. When the western end of the Link Road is completed in 1978, the site will assume a greater prominence by reason of the increased volume of through-traffic which will then use the road.

Boundaries

The north and west boundaries are road curtilages, the east boundary is the sports complex and the south boundary is a main services corridor containing an electricity cable and two water pipes.

Constraints

All of the existing ironworks slag must be redeployed within the site boundary. The opportunity exists to divert the watercourse on the west side of the heap, if required. Ground levels along the existing services corridor must be maintained. A quantity of topsoil, at present located on land immediately to the south, is available for use on the site. All other soil requirements will have to be met by importation. Competitors should attempt to take full advantage of the 100% grants available from the Department of the Environment for work falling within their definition of approved reclamation. Access for working the site may be off the A6074 Road at a point to be determined, or off Merrington Lane along the access track. The main access to the site after completion of the scheme will be from the existing playing fields. Work must commence on site early in 1978.

Requirements

The site is to form an extension to the adjacent sports complex. While competitors have the freedom to suggest a range of different facilities, these should include at least one 100 metres × 64 metres soccer pitch and basic provision for spectators. The site should be sheltered from northerly and westerly directions.

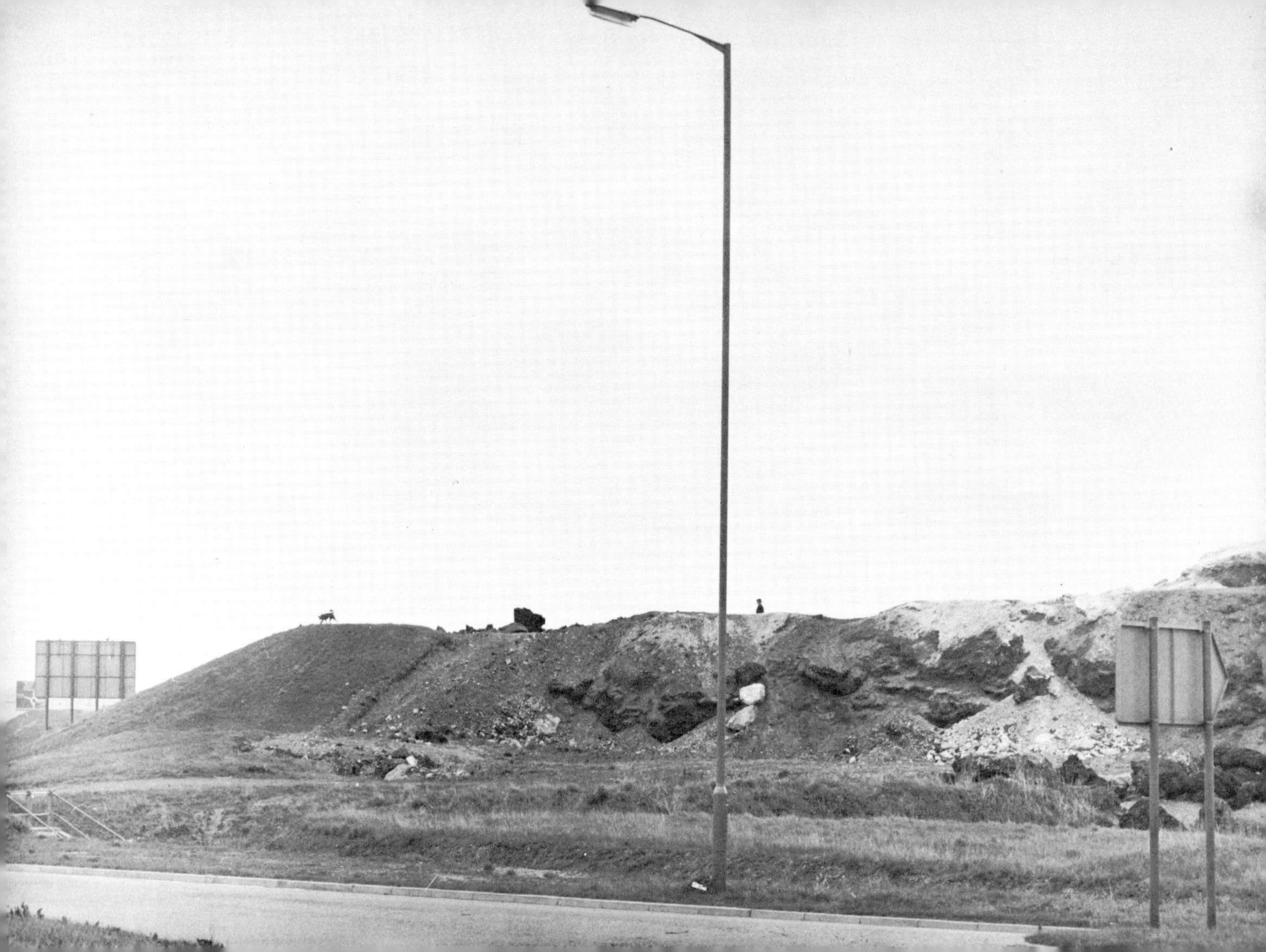

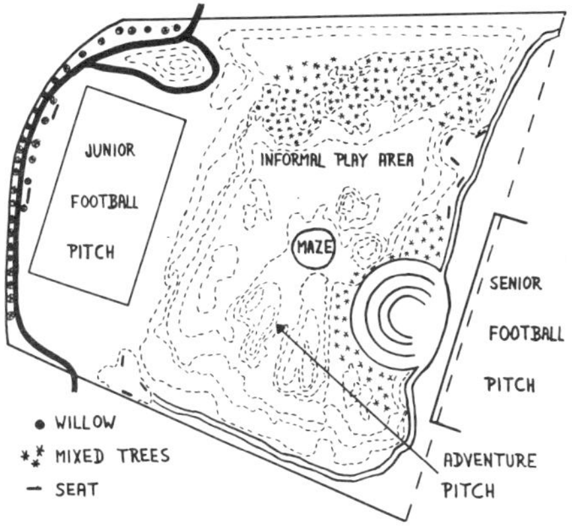

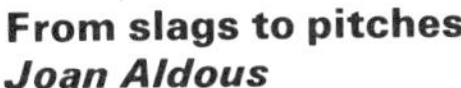

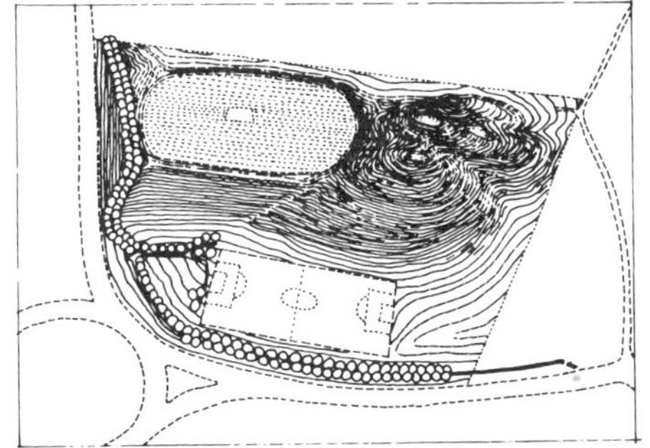

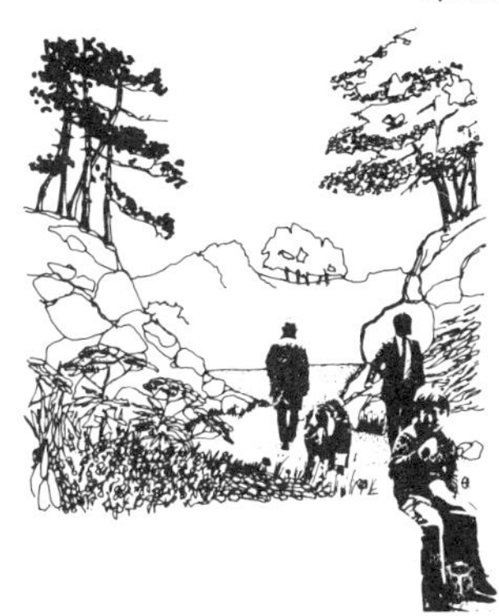

From slags to pitches
Joan Aldous

The proposed scheme is designed to provide recreation facilities for as wide an age range as possible. It aims to make good the lack of informal play facilities in the town centre area by incorporating two football pitches, a pleasant walkway with sitting areas for mothers with young children, an amphitheatre and an 'adventure pitch' (playground), including a maze, bumpy cycle tracks, structures made of railway sleepers and old tyres and a jumping pit. The scheme is designed to move as little slag as possible, make full use of existing contours, and use cheap materials where appropriate.

Born 1938 in London. Studied at Reading University. Senior lecturer in mathematics at the Open University.

Slagheap hillscape
David Graham

The slagheaps make the site prominent in relation to adjacent areas and their scale remains an important element, but their appearance is improved. They should remain a feature to be appreciated in the landscape from a distance and which will create simple shapes for activities related to adjacent facilities. The theme of the traditionally pleasing landscape elements of man-made mounds is developed using the outer slopes to view adjacent formal sports and raised perimeter terraces, surrounding a flat-topped cricket field. An additional element, influenced by turf mazes and the labyrinthine approaches to ancient mounds, is to retain the three existing peaks of the slagheaps within a maze following their contours. An avenue of trees is proposed combining with the diverted stream to effect a softening of the edges of the site. It is intended that grassed slopes would be supplemented with hardy ground cover.

Born 1948. Studied architecture at Manchester University. Works as architect.

Spennymoor reclamation
Edward Hutchison, Anthony Warren

1. Concept: use the potential in the slag heap.
2. Recreation: (i) a sheltered multi-use pitch with touchline and higher level viewing; (ii) a wild flower walk through a combination of crags and rich underplanted woodland clumps and the diverted and enhanced stream with marginal aquatic planting; (iii) a cycle track.
3. Implementation: (i) concentrating effort and money in 'ecozones' of rich and substantial mature planting; (ii) retaining the best crags, foundry lava and clean screes as a contrast into which the planting will spread; (iii) maximum use of job creation, school and youth club projects to reduce the risk of vandalism and save money; (iv) use soft material supplemented with pockets of richer planting.

Edward Hutchison born 1946 in Fife. Studied at Kingston College of Art, the Royal College of Art and Thames Polytechnic. Works as landscape architect.

Anthony Warren born 1940 in Exeter. Studied at the Welsh School of Architecture and the University of Strathclyde. Works as architect.

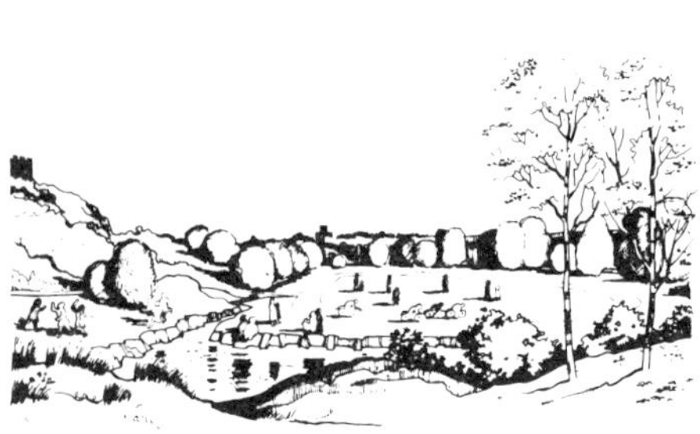

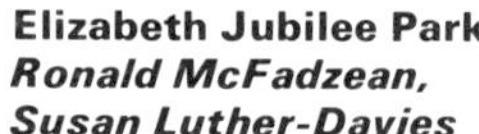

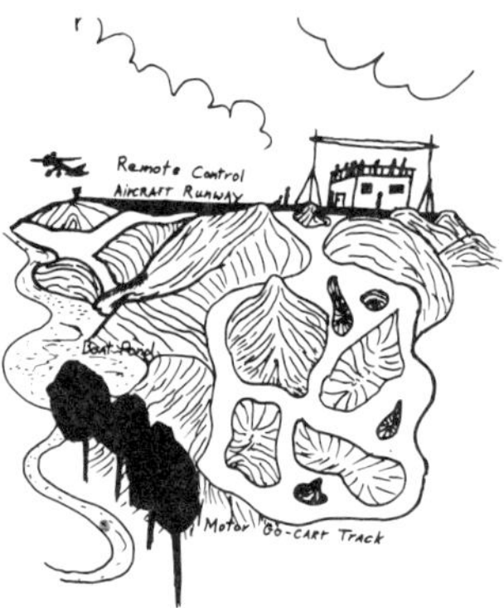

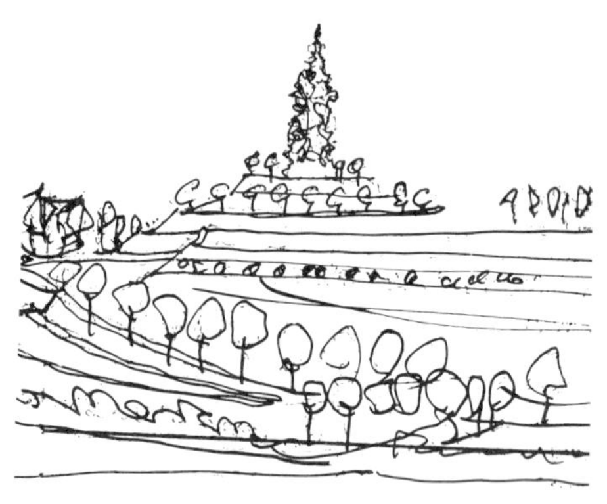

Elizabeth Jubilee Park
Ronald McFadzean,
Susan Luther-Davies

The key to the design is Jubilee Castle. It is built of railway sleepers on top of the highest part of the site and commemorates the festivities of 1977. The escarpment on which it stands is called Bessemer Ridge after the great ironworks which once stood on the site. It provides a viewing and kite-flying area. To the north is Beacon Hill which forms a bonfire site for Guy Fawkes Night and firework displays. To the east of the castle is the Highland Park, a vast parade ground. It provides a football pitch which can be used in summer for the Spennymoor Highland Games and by the local drum majorettes. To the south of the park is an open-air theatre constructed of grassed earth terraces.

Ronald McFadzean born 1932. Studied architecture in Glasgow, Strathclyde and Sheffield. Works as architect and planner.

Susan Luther-Davies born 1946. Studied in Exeter, Newcastle and Glasgow. Works as landscape designer and lecturer.

Aero port
Nicholas Rae

The slagheap is used as a small mountain range with tracks in the valleys for motorised go-carts. At the highest point there is a tarmac runway for remote-controlled model petrol aeroplanes and a building for storage and controls. The stream is made into a pond for model boats. There is a car park and a café.
Born in 1965. Attends King Alfred's School, London.

Spenny heights
T J M Reynolds

The driving force behind this scheme is to demonstrate how the main disadvantages of any area can be turned to good account. At Spennymoor the plateau-like character will be retained, only changing the heights of the west side by dozing tracks and rough terracing upwards while the east and south side will be dozed downwards. This has the effect of giving shelter from prevailing winds. Not the least important consideration is protection from vandalism later. The greatest defence against this is to involve the schoolchildren and young unemployed, and for this reason I suggested a glass tower principally made of bottles which would give great lightweight and structural strength. I have also suggested easily planted flora, either naturally resilient or, as for example berberis, not only beautiful but well armed with natural spiky protection.

Born 1933 in Brighton. Rome Scholar. Works as painter and wine merchant.

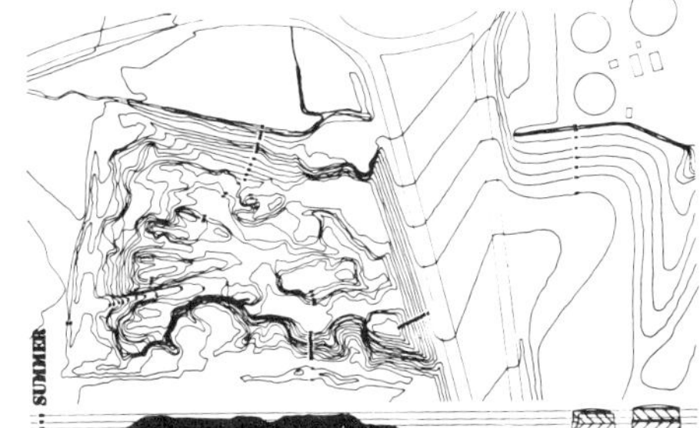

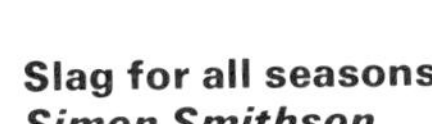

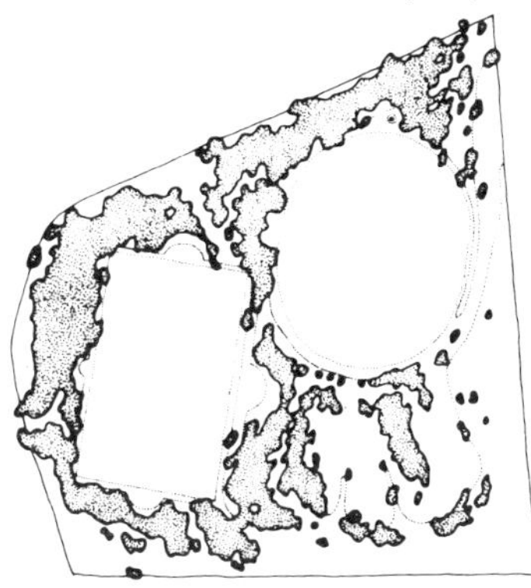

The Slaggie Eleven
A M Smithson

The heroes of the Spennymoor Slagheap are formed of up-ended conglomerates of slag painted in bright stripes of colour borrowed from local teams, both amateur and professional, as follows: Spennymoor: shirt, black/white vertical stripes, pants black; Crook Town: shirt amber, black collar, pants black; Willington: shirt blue/white vertical stripes, pants blue; W Auckland: shirt all white, amber collar, pants white; Durham City: shirt amber, pants blue; Stanley: shirt red/white vertical stripes, pants black; Hartlepool United: shirt blue, pants white. The slaggie heroes are randomly positioned on the crestline of the bowl which provides a protected pitch. The encircling surfaces are graded for ease of maintenance and would be seeded with grass. Certain hollows, reminders of Spennymoor's industrial labours, will be planted with Biting Stonecrop to flower with yellow stars May—July. Trees are planted round the watercourse which has been brought to circle slightly further to the west.
Born 1928. Works as architect in private practice.

Slag for all seasons
Simon Smithson

A coat of many colours covers the slag heap; four-metre-high stripes of grasses and wild flowers wrap around the heap. The grasses and flowers have been chosen for their ability to grow in poor conditions, minimising the need for soil improvement, especially near the top. A attempt has been made to choose plants that might attract back to Durham those butterflies that must have filled the air of the North East in the time of Thomas Bewick. The proposed flowers and plants are mat grass, heather, thyme to attract the grayling butterfly; blue moor grass, birdsfoot trefoil—common blue butterfly; flattened meadow grass, heath dog violet—pearl bordered fritillary; cocks-foot grass, common poppy—wall butterfly; annual meadow grass, hemlock—brown argus butterfly; common cotton grass—large heath butterfly.
Born 1954 in London. Works in an architect's office.

Stuff the genius loci?
Derek Walker Associates

We hope that this and our schemes for briefs 5, 7, 10 and 12 show a consistent attitude to landscape design: the common factor is a kind of simplicity which we feel is appropriate at the moment. The appropriateness does not for us lie primarily in the comparative cheapness of the proposals we show, though in the present economic circumstances cheapness may be virtue enough. Neither do we aim for a rarified esoteric simplicity. Instead we feel that most 'modern landscape design' is over elaborate, over designed, fussy and tries to do too much, with too many materials, too obtrusively. Obvious solutions are ignored. We feel that the tradition of urban landscape (and all the projects are urban) was one of robust simplicity—a tradition to which we would like to return.

Scheme 1

We moved mountains to meet the brief and provide a football pitch and cricket square. The most interesting parts of the site are retained and the slopes stabilised and topsoiled. The areas would be afforested with the residual budget. As earthmoving accounts for the major

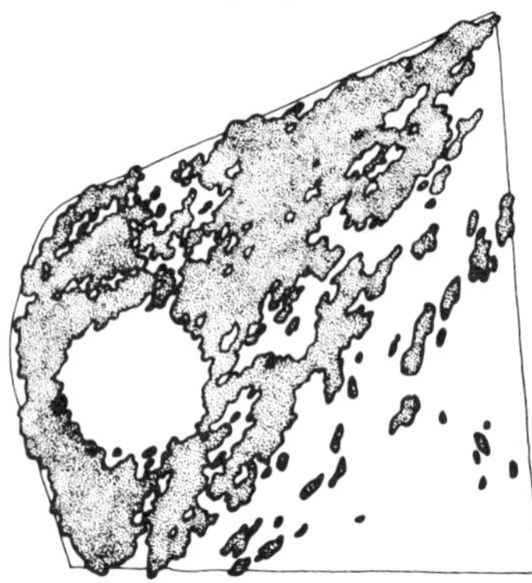

part· of the expenditure, we tended to look also at an alternative design option.
Scheme 2
Why vandalise the site in the name of sport? A much simpler and cheaper scheme would exploit the potential of the site by minimal disturbance. The stabilisation and topsoiling of the slopes could lead to a rich afforestation. Surely the slagheap would have more uses as a wooded grassy 'mountain' than as a playing field extension? An investment for the future? A Jubilee monument? Or an industrial monument?
Architectural practice.

Roundabout at Ware

Town into Country – Gateway to the historic town of Ware

The centre of the site is a large roundabout junction fitted into the old street pattern at the junction of Wadesmill Road, Baldock Street and Watton Road, which was carried out when the main north-south route was the A.10 trunk road. The A.10 has since been re-routed outside Ware. The site forms the northern entry into the historic centre of Ware by way of Baldock Street and the land slopes gently to the south. The site comprises three parts:

1. A roundabout island (approximately 38 metres diameter) and 2 small triangular traffic islands on the north and west approaches. Proposals within these areas should not overhang the highway and be set back a minimum of 600 mm from the kerb. On the two islands, there should be no obstruction to drivers' visibility.

2. A triangular site on the north-west of the roundabout, 140 metres long by a maximum of 40 metres wide, bounded on the west side by the back gardens of houses at a higher level on a retaining wall along the boundary up to 4 metres high. This wall is a combination of a number of different constructions and is scarred by structures since removed. It is certainly of no beauty.

3. A public car park approximately 60 metres × 50 metres on the east side of the roundabout bounded on the north by Coronation Road which does not connect to the roundabout for vehicles.

The site is also bounded by a petrol filling station and garage in the north-east corner, displaying typical garage advertisements, and by Baldock Street on the south which is closely defined by two-storey buildings built directly on to the narrow footpaths, many of the buildings being of architectural importance. This street leads directly into High Street.

Aim of Project

To restore, to the northern end of Baldock Street, a scale better related to the buildings in the centre of Ware and to their inhabitants instead of the present scale of motor vehicles, and to create a fitting entrance to an historic town of national importance.

Restraints

Although the roundabout does not now carry trunk road traffic, it is still busy and it is the County Council's intention to further reduce traffic in Baldock Street and High Street by constructing a relief road which would leave this roundabout in an easterly direction through the centre of the car park (3.). This would require a total highway width of 12–14 metres. This road is not yet programmed for construction. The triangular area (2.) represents land left over after the construction of the roundabout and it is the County Council's intention that this area should be developed. The most suitable use would be flats or an hotel. This site is, however, likely to be expensive to develop and for that reason, may remain vacant for a number of years. The car park (3.) will remain in this use at least until the relief road is constructed and proposals for this should therefore incorporate a continued use for car parking purposes.

Proposals

Taking account of the aims and constraints of this site, proposals should:

1. Produce fairly rapid results.

2. Produce a scheme centred on the roundabout and backed up by proposals for the triangular area and the car park, bearing in mind that proposals on these areas may have a limited life.

3. Be relatively inexpensive, bearing in mind the limited life of a major part of the site before it is re-developed.

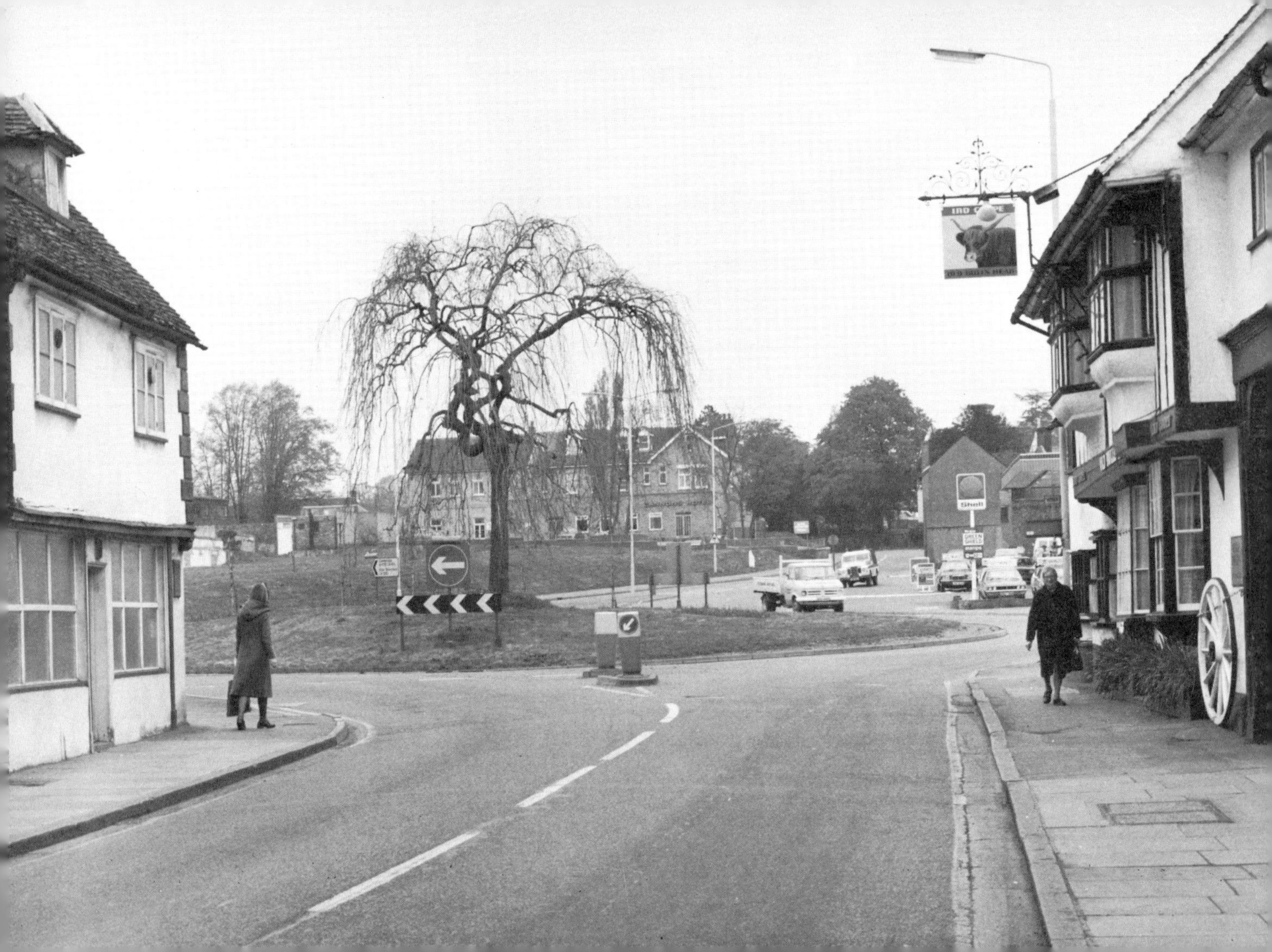
OLD GREEN HEAD
OLD GREEN HEAD
Shell
GREEN
SHIELD

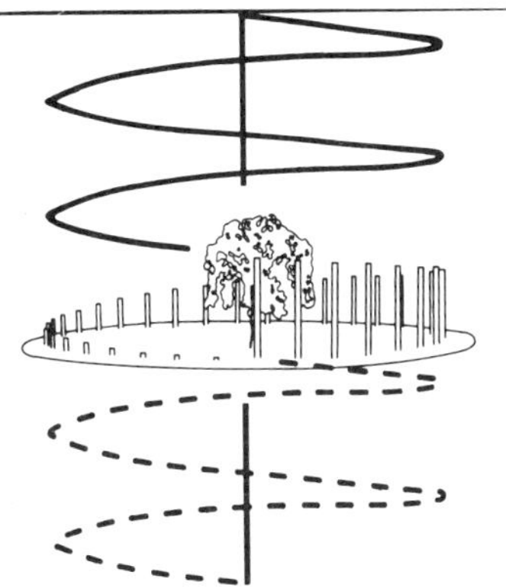

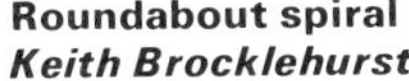

Roundabout spiral
Keith Brocklehurst

This evolves from my interest in the use and philosophy of yantras, stone circles and other related devices for 'centring' the individual. The roundabout island would have 36 wooden poles around its circumference, spaced 1.5 m apart and increasing in height from 0.2 m to 7.2 m in a clockwise direction. Twenty-five wooden poles would be placed on the nw triangular site in a predominantly n–s configuration, the height decreasing south to north from 2 m to 4 m. The boundary wall would be painted red and dark green, changes in the design corresponding with the ground plan changes delineated by the poles. The car park would contain 4 units each made up of two wooden poles jointed at an angle of 20 degrees. The height to the apex of the poles increases from 6 m to 6.6 m furthest from the roundabout, the units to be set astride a west-east line that passes through the centre of the roundabout.

Born 1946 in Cheshire. Studied at Leicester College of Art, Chelsea School of Art and the Slade School of Fine Art. Taught at Leicester Polytechnic 1969–74.

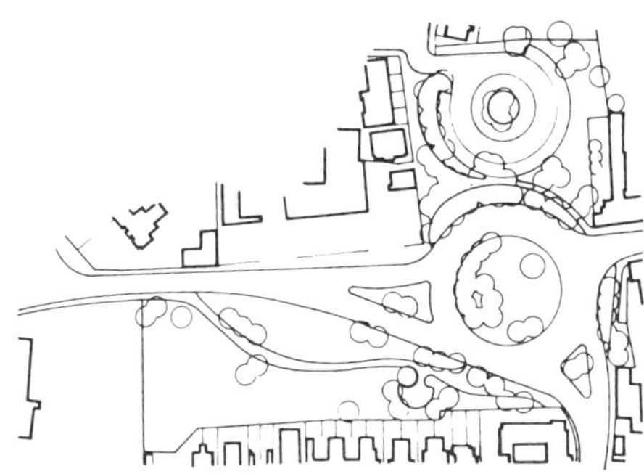

Market roundabout
R D Caddick

The roundabout retains most of its existing trees whose form is reinforced with ground shaping and planting. The triangular site is recontoured and planted to provide an internal pedestrian walk. A soft grass area intended for public use is proposed to the north. A hard area with seating is located in a sheltered recess close to the south entrance. High brick planters define public routes except where the planter retaining walls merge into the ground to encourage public use of grass areas. The car park is retained in a radial form, providing an area not only for cars but possibly a weekly market. The pedestrian route is taken away from the road between brick planters and an arcade of trees to a meeting place in front of the local shop. Trees and shrub planters provide insulation between existing houses and the car park.

Born 1953 in Warrington, Cheshire. Studies at Canterbury School of Art, School of Architecture.

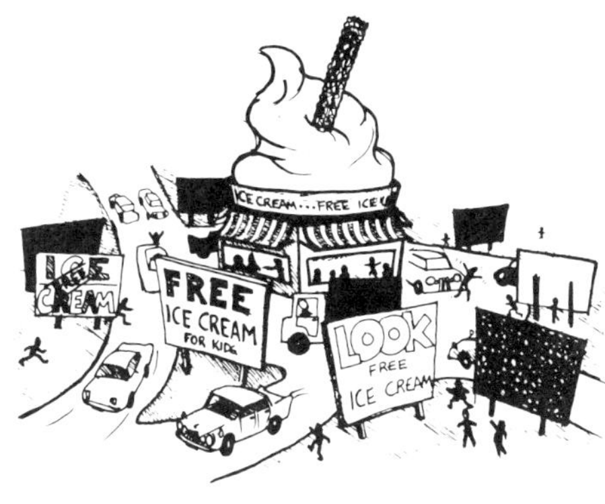

Ice-sore at Ware
Oska Crossly

What Ware needs on this roundabout is an ice cream shop, giving ice cream away to kids. Large signs around it could advertise it and also obscure drivers' vision. Roads should be widened to increase speed and amount of traffic. Kids will love the adventure of dancing between speeding cars to get the ice cream. Those that make it can sit at the large windows, stuff themselves sick and laugh at other kids trying to cross.

Born 1952 in Ware. Has worked as a coalman and postman and is now unemployed.

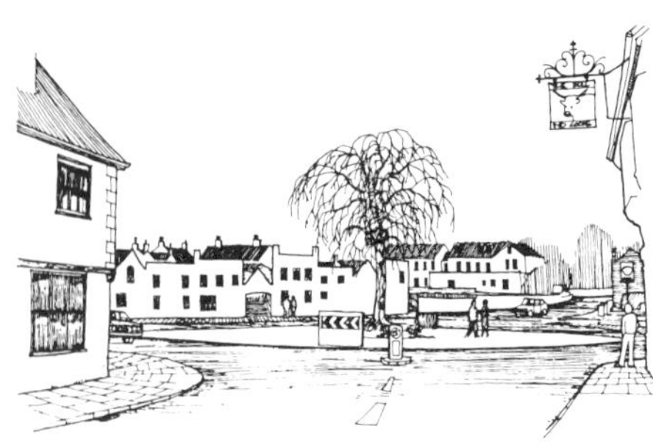

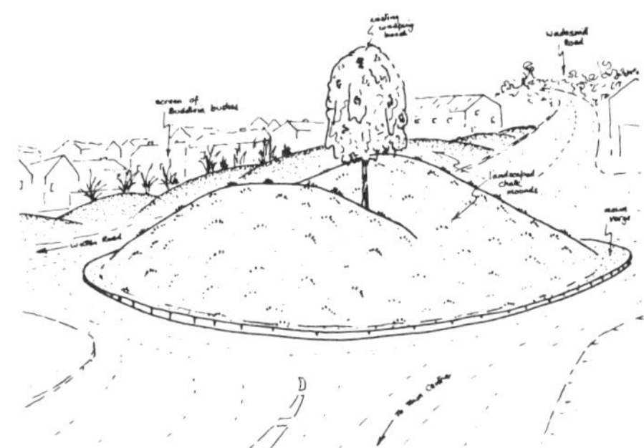

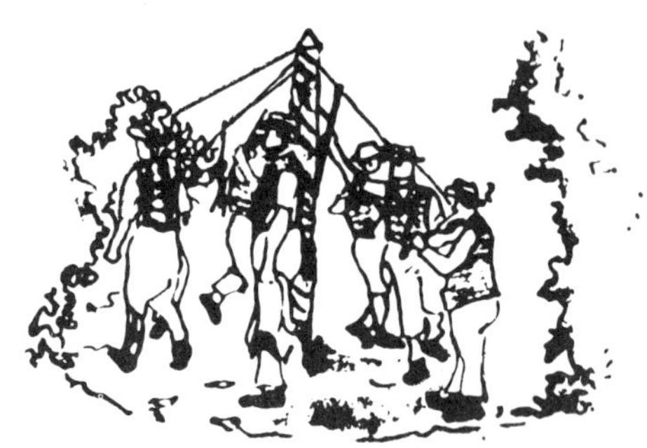

Instant townscape
John Donnelly, C J Grasby

The intention is to recreate a space suitable to the historic character of Ware in an area which has been blighted by clearance. It was felt that a temporarily built form should be recreated on the site to restore lost enclosure. Instead of the scheme being centred on the roundabout we have made the roundabout the centre of a new space. The stage-set nature of the new facades is deliberately emphasised by leaving them as abstract white screens, but detail such as doors and windows is formed by cut-outs providing visual interest and an appropriate scale. Gateways and arches provide access to car parks etc. behind, so that the facades are used in a 3-dimensional way.

John Donnelly born 1950 in Clacton. Studied architecture at Nottingham University.

C J Grasby born 1952 in Manchester. Studied architecture at Sheffield University. Both work for Basildon New Town Development Corporation

A chalk downland habitat
J C Doyle

Over the past ten years a 'chalk garden' has been established at our school with the following aims in view: 1) to develop a technique for producing an easily maintained landscape feature as an alternative to the traditional flower beds; 2) to aid the conservation of the increasingly rare chalk downland plants; 3) to serve as a teaching aid.

We have tried to simulate chalk downland, short turf, by a combination of selected seed and carefully timed grass cutting. The success can perhaps be judged by the fact that wild orchids and cowslips are amongst the plants flourishing in the habitat. The attractiveness, cheapness of construction and ease of management of such a habitat would, we feel, lend itself to the enhancement of wasteland. We suggest that a series of landscaped chalk banks be constructed on the roundabout by school children and council workers.

Born in 1938 in Hertford. Studied geology at University of Hull. Teaches biology, geology and conservation work at Hadham Hall School, Hertfordshire.

St Vitus' Dance
Elaine Fade

To enhance a blank space which includes Ware roundabout and surroundings it was felt that the area required a more intense definition and a sense of enclosure. The northern approach to Baldock roundabout needs a well-landscaped treatment and a 'focal point' to mark the approach to the historic country town of Ware. The area around Baldock roundabout would be landscaped with trees, grass, etc., and the road changed to cobblestones and bricks, provision being made for traffic to be diverted in the future. The green islands would become the 'village green' around the Morris Men Roundabout where various social acitivites could take place. Focused on the roundabout would be a large pool, enclosed by greenery, with the group of Morris Men dancing around a maypole fountain in brightly coloured costumes.

Born 1952 in Taunton, Somerset. Studies interior design at Middlesex Polytechnic.

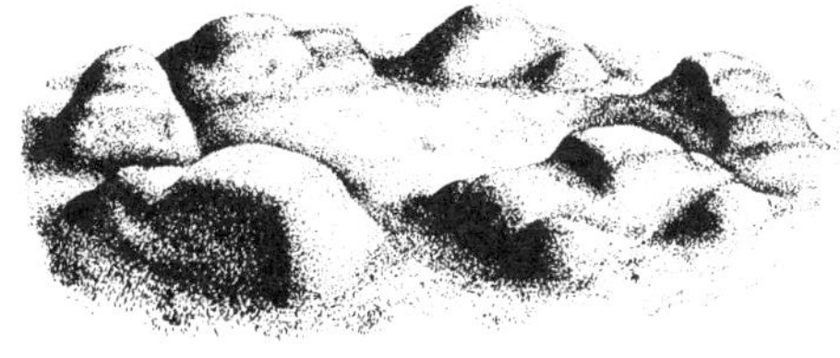

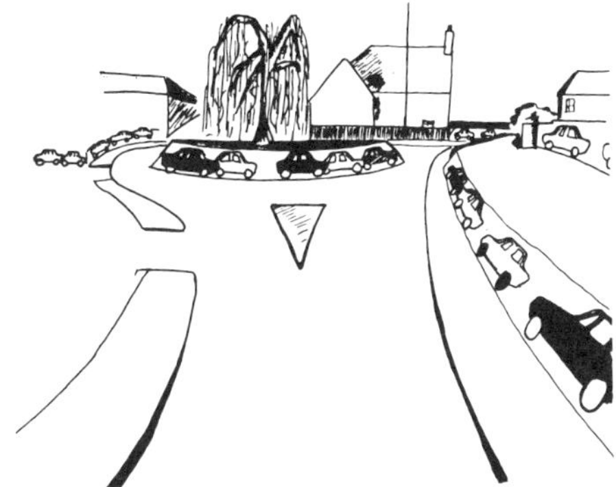

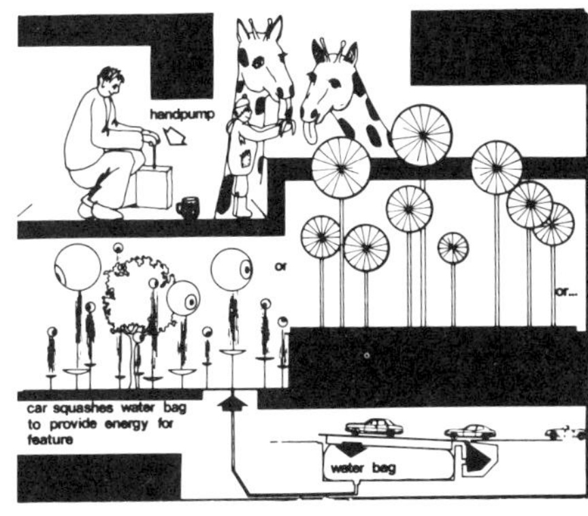

Grassed-in
Tim Gwyther

A roundabout is a singularly isolated part of the environment. Cut off from the rest of the landscape, it is an artificial and virtually inaccessable no-man's-land which exists solely for the benefit of the motorist: a region to be orbited, never traversed. This proposal which stems from the premise that art can become the landscape rather than be placed upon it as a separate entity, features a number of grass-covered vehicles arranged around the perimeter of the site and represents a means whereby the roundabout can make some direct reference to the circumstances which created it.

Born 1948 in Woking, Surrey. Studied at Stourbridge Art College, Birmingham and Brighton Polytechnics. Teaches graphics in a sixth form college.

Redesigned roundabout
Simon Balle School

The site has undistinguished skylines in almost all directions made up of mainly low and uninteresting buildings. There is a feeling of clutter and congestion caused by walls disfigured by demolition of previous buildings and the presence of numerous cars in the car park and in the area of the garage, causing a clutter of shapes along the entire east end of the site. Our plan is to use the silhouette of the motor car for securing a greater feeling of unity and cohesion in the scene. In places where it is not possible to erect or paint, the motif trees will be planted to hide unsightly areas caused by demolition and dereliction. This makes a virtue of the chief cause of the clutter—the motor car— and therefore makes them less noticeable.

Tim Morley and Mark Fell born 1962, Andrew Whitaker born 1963 in Hertford. Attend Simon Balle School, Hertford.

Multifarious developments
Oakeley Turner Bate-Williams

The site is essentially dynamic in that its existence is caused by movement, so the proposal is to provide some form of dynamic feature for the roundabout, whose motive force would be supplied by the passage of motor vehicles through the site. In this way the motor vehicle helps to restore the balance which it has been allowed to upset. The main proposal is that hinged pressure plates acting upon reservoirs of water be let into the road: vehicles passing over the plates will pump water to the feature on the roundabout. Subsidiary proposals: i) make a storeyard for building materials and construction plant to the north west of the roundabout; stored materials could be used to create an adventure playground with a giraffe house. ii) provide handpumps at suitable pedestrian points and adjacent to the Public House south east of the roundabout, so that everyone can join in the fun. There are many ways of using the water, some of them are explored in the entry.

For biographical notes see catalogue number 91.

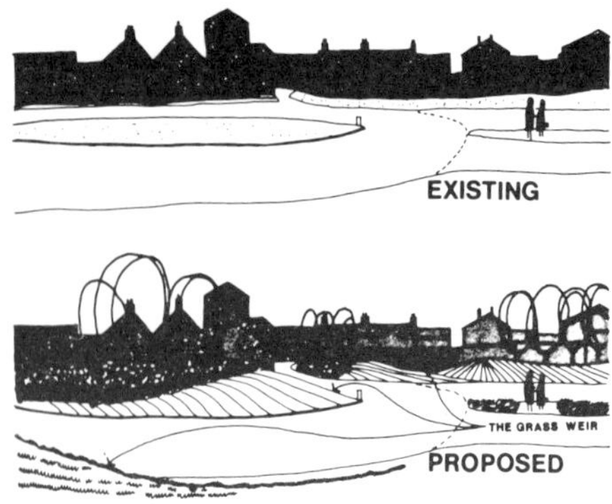

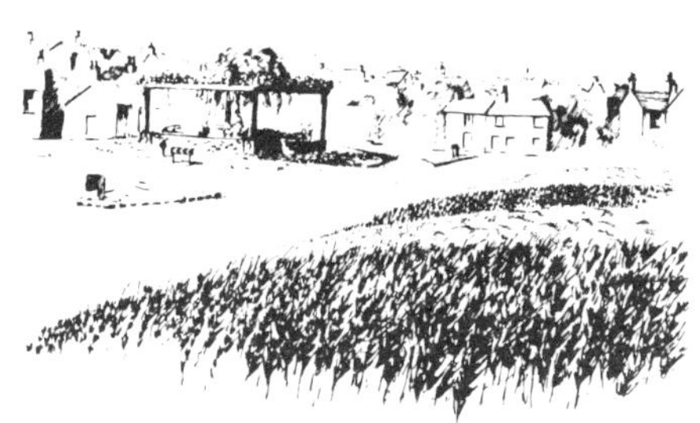

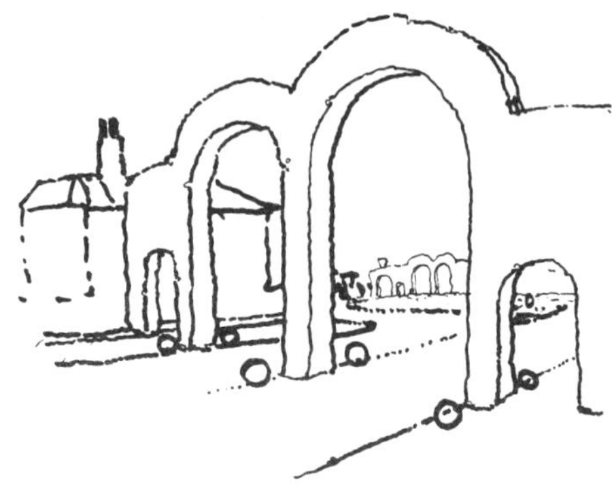

A grass weir for Ware
Tom Turner, Margaret Hogg

The reason why Ware appears to sprawl into the countryside as you approach the town is the lack of clear gateways between town and country. A rural-urban barrier is needed. The roundabout can form part of it as a visual weir between pools of rural and urban character. A 'grass weir', made of carefully shaped and mown grass banks set in a framework of trees and shrubs, symbolises the weir from which the name 'Ware' is derived. The original weir was constructed by the Danes to protect their ships; King Alfred stranded them by draining the river, and his son Edward built a town here. The mounds can be built of waste earth from local building projects and fertilized with waste culmns from the local maltings. Most of the funds should be spent on grass seeding and tree planting.

Tom Turner born 1946. Studied social science at St Andrews and landscape design in Edinburgh.

Margaret Hogg born 1948. Studied landscape design in Leeds. Both work as landscape architects.

The Elizabethan Great Bed of Ware
Peter Vickers, Mick Coleshaw

One of Ware's most tangible links with the past is the 16th Century carved oak Great Bed of Ware which stands in Jacobean panelled splendour in the Victoria and Albert Museum. Unfortunately no monument to Ware's linen generosity to its Elizabethan visitors can be seen in the town. The proposal is to erect a large brick and terracotta four-posted sculpture on the island. The intricate carving of the original bed will be represented by a wealth of climbing and trailing plants, whilst the 'bedspread' will be created by a formal garden laid out in quilt patterns. It is proposed to continue the historical theme by treating the adjacent triangular site as a medieval three field system. Undulating fallow rows will be interspersed with strips of oil seed rape, poppies, wheat and barley

Peter Vickers born 1947 in Misterton, Nottinghamshire. Studied at Leeds College of Art and the Royal College of Art. Teaches at Trent Polytechnic.

Mick Coleshaw born 1948 in Nottingham. Studies furniture design at Trent Polytechnic.

Circular hedge
David Walker

The project shows the roundabout enclosed by a massive yew hedge. The centre of the hedge coincides with the centre of the roundabout. The hedge is cut and shaped to allow the passage of cars and pedestrians. Within the larger circle there is dense groundcover planting which is highly fragrant and predominantly silver in colour. Cars and pedestrians brushing past provide an antidote to traffic fumes. The large circular space is conceived as a barbican or an ante-chamber to the town. The appearance of the hedge is such that the buildings appear to interrupt its total form rather than vice versa.

Born 1940 in Tredegar, South Wales. Studied at RWA School of Architecture Bristol and University of Bristol. Teaches architecture at Gloucestershire College of Art and Design.

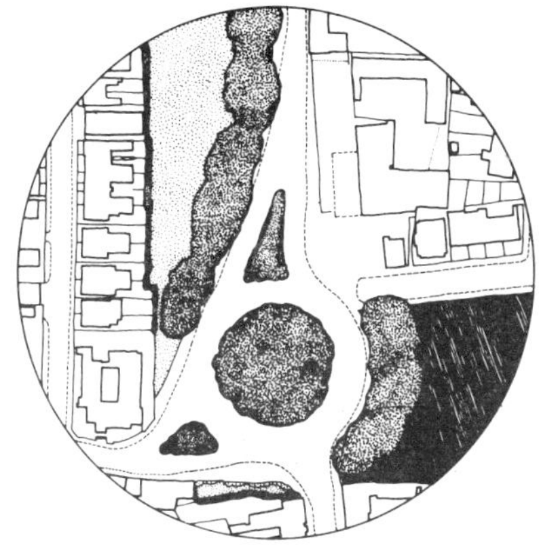

Stuff the genius loci?
Derek Walker Associates

It seemed imperative to form a landscape structure that could be retained regardless of the form that future developments on parts of this site might take, and to produce a planting solution for those areas with a permanent, unchanging function. We propose planting the roundabout with trees and ground cover species to give an attractive stop to Baldock Street, and a low wall, in brick or local stone, to surround the roundabout incorporating directional signs. The two traffic islands would be similarly raised on a low wall and planted with ground cover. Circular directional signs would be post mounted and set in these islands. The larger triangular area to the north west of the junction would be graded and seeded and the retaining wall covered with both evergreen and freely flowering climbing plants, with a double row of trees along the inside edge of the pavement. If development does not occur for several years, a degree of maturity in the planting would be an asset.

Architectural practice.

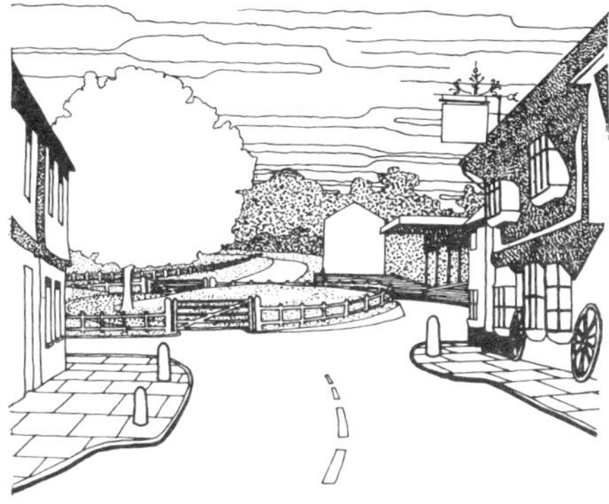

Edge Ware Road
Graham Waterhouse

1 Tidy up the old A ten
    Give it self respect again.
    Hide away old Ware's worst scars,
    Still used now for parking cars.
2 Site signs and lamps with utmost care,
    And need those traffic isles be there?
    (If Engineers are thus non-plussed,
    It's sure to please the Civic Trust.)
3 Pick out lines with fences rural.
    Imitate one on a mural.
    Give Ware Town an edge anew!
    Have a gateway—No! Have two!

It marks a boundary as grassland and winding road are seen beyond the wattle and daub; gates and fences add to the impression of countryside. The brick walls reduce the area to one which may be perceived at once without confusion, and Baldock Street no longer has a lonely and amputated look.

Born 1950 in Houghton, Cambridgeshire. Studied at University College Bartlett School of Architecture. Works as architect.

Kelvingrove Art Gallery and Museum

A new approach

The Kelvingrove Art Gallery and Museum is a listed building and was a successful competition design by the Architects Sir J W Simpson and Milner Allen with external sculpture by Sir George Frampton. It was built from 1892 to 1900 for the Glasgow International Exhibition of 1901 when Glasgow was generally regarded as the second City in the Empire. On one side the dark red sandstone building faces the University of Glasgow across the River Kelvin and the well wooded Kelvin Glen, but seen from busy Argyle Street the building is at its most grandiose and impressive.

The terrace

The terrace was originally laid out as a flat area at a lower level than the floor of the building and with a simple and formal arrangement of lawns, paths and trees, enclosed at each end by walls as an extension of the building. At present the terrace has matching elm tree at each side of the main entrance path, another a little further along and four other ornamental trees of small size, all of which can be transplanted elsewhere. Into the lawns has unsuccessfully been introduced six circular flower beds and two lighting columns with overhead cables. The paths have deteriorated and resurfacing is required if they are to remain. Well established holly hedges at each end of the terrace and along the upper access road provide added height to the walls and as a strong piece of structural planting are probably worth retaining. The difference in levels between terrace and building, the "weight" of the building, steps and walls, and the length and width of the central path combine in scale to reduce the approaching visitor to diminutive proportions and emphasise the impressiveness of the building.

The collection

Kelvingrove Art Gallery and Museum houses one of the finest civic art collections in Britain, particularly strong in 19th century French painting. The decorative art collection is also important and includes pottery, porcelain and glass from most of the important factories. The arms and armour collection is perhaps second only to that in the Tower of London. The archaeological gallery displays the story of man from earliest times and examines classical sites as well as the archaeology of Scotland. The Scottish History gallery brings this story up to modern times. Important ethnographical collections meanwhile illustrate other cultures. Part of the Museum is devoted to the natural history of Scotland. Geological history, mammals, birds and fishes from all the areas of Scotland are illustrated and new displays in preparation will introduce the visitor to Scotland's splendid scenery and wildlife.

The competition brief

1. The terrace might be considered a very prominent shop window and as an extension of the art gallery and museum building.

2. The dignity of the terrace should be maintained and designs should be sympathetic to the architecture as a whole, and provide interest, an invitation and welcome to visitors to the Museum.

3. Being on the south side of the Building, the terrace is both sunny and sheltered and sitting areas might be provided.

4. Good access must be maintained between bus stops and footpaths along Argyle Street and the steps leading to the main entrance to the building.

5. The existing secondary path system, lawns and flower beds may be removed or altered and the wide main asphalt path leading to the main entrance to the building, may be altered, providing item 4 is observed.

6. The terrace could be subject to vandalism and therefore any designs should be fairly robust.

7. At night, low pressure sodium lighting from four masts highlight the building facade. Competitors might consider that complementary or other lighting could be used to good effect, perhaps as a changing feature within the terrace area.

8. Materials used in the construction of a prize-winning scheme should be readily obtainable and relatively inexpensive.

9. The design should provide a permanent basic construction but allow flexibility in use. A platform for temporary display purposes may be considered and some sculpture and geological exhibits could be made available for this purpose.

10. An important design criteria could be to encourage the employment under the Job Creation Programme of unemployed and variously skilled artists, craftsmen, tradesmen and artisans in such ways that skill, manual dexterity and pride of workmanship will give ultimate job satisfaction and impart to the public a sense of achievement, interest and respect.

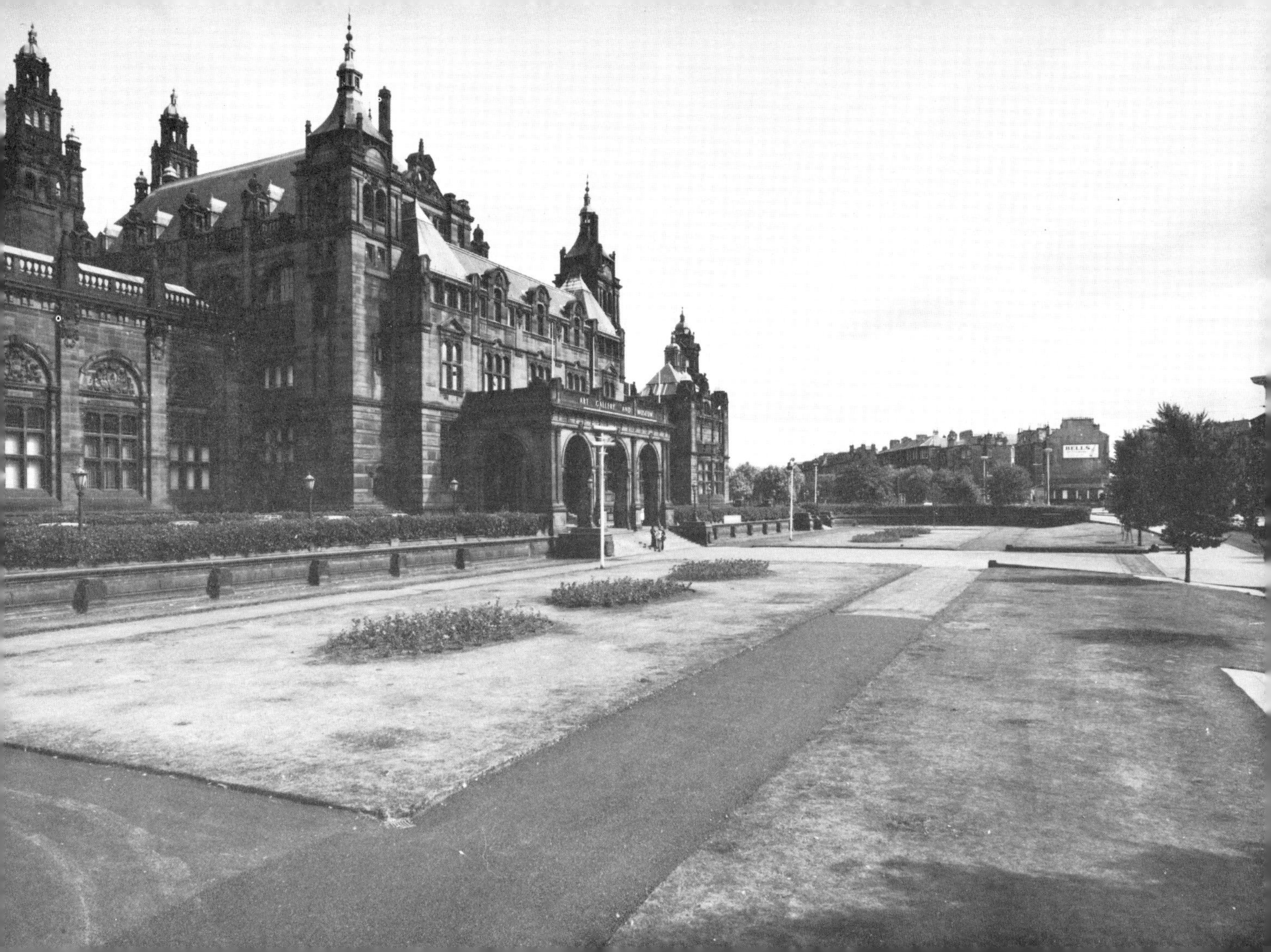

ART GALLERY AND MUSEUM
BELLS

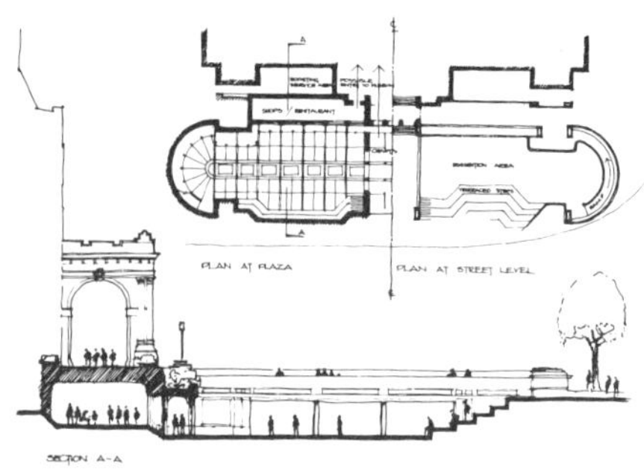

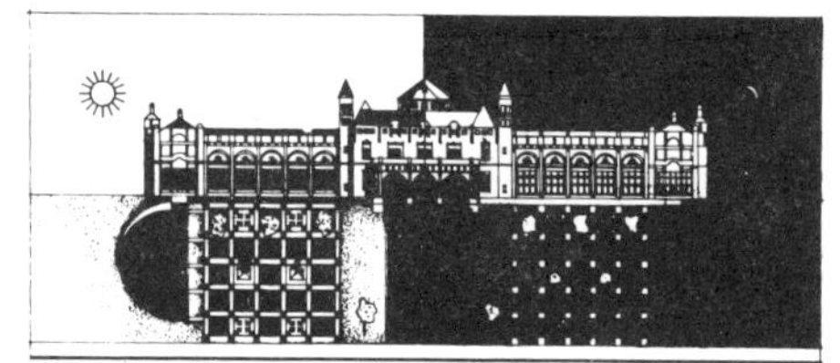

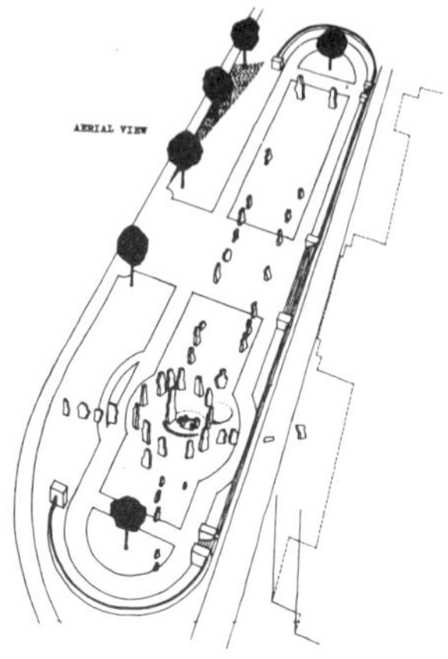

Flexible multi-purpose space
Barrie Briscoe

Concept: Below ground level paved courtyard (exhibition space) with terraced access from road and direct access to lower ground level of museum building and ramp access to and from the entrance level. The ideal would be matching stone with the existing building, but at this stage it is the intention to use concrete, with attention to detailing and workmanship. The terraced steps will be timber edged with turf treads. Courtyards are to be paved with blocks, or coloured road type surface with decorative block patterning. Suggested uses: changing exhibits, public participation programmes, museum displays, craft stalls for local artists/artisans; museum/art gallery shop, bazaars, theatre (with temporary/mobile thrust stage), sculpture garden, licensed restaurant, café. Attributes: orientation to the sun, protection from the wind. Grass terracing and courtyards are inviting to the public.

Born in 1936 in Gloucester. Studied architecture and painting in the USA. Works as architect, artist and designer.

Tartan grid
Helen Brown

I propose a formal, symmetrical landscape for a formal, symmetrical building, but incorporating an element of naive fantasy in response to the fairytale quality of the building. The level of the ground is raised to the level of the top of the existing retaining wall, and gradually returns to pavement level in a series of stepped terraces. The steps at each change in level would provide good casual seating. The hard landscaping is laid out in the form of a tartan grid of paving slabs delineating squares containing various types of surface treatment and activity, including tables and chairs for summer teas, trees, display stands for sculpture or exhibits, and planting boxes. At the intersection points of the grid lines, pavement lights would give sparkle and magic at night. This theme of grid and pattern is an extension of the gallery interior where the floors are paved with geometric tiled patterns.

Born 1951 in London. Studied architecture at Edinburgh University. Works as architectural assistant.

Kelvingrove/Callanish
William Chaitkin

The proposal is to reproduce the megalithic monument Callanish, full size, in concrete casts of the original stones. The dramatic presence of its processional avenue, stone circle, central menhir and chambered cairn, on a series of earth mounds, exchanges an evocative but remote setting for public spatial experience. To fit the Kelvingrove site, the replica's orientation has been shifted 40°W. If the Scottish scholar, Alexander Thom, is correct in identifying it as the lunar observatory of an astronomical cult, its ancient builders may have chosen the northernmost of the Outer Hebrides for its high latitude, so the alignments would not, in any case, work at Glasgow. Probably dating from about 1800 BC, Callanish remains one of the most important of such monuments in Britain—evidently more accurately laid out, older and in a finer state of preservation than Stonehenge III. Let it be seen.

Born 1942. Studied architecture and art history at Washington University, St. Louis, USA. Lectures at the Central School of Art and Chelsea School of Art.

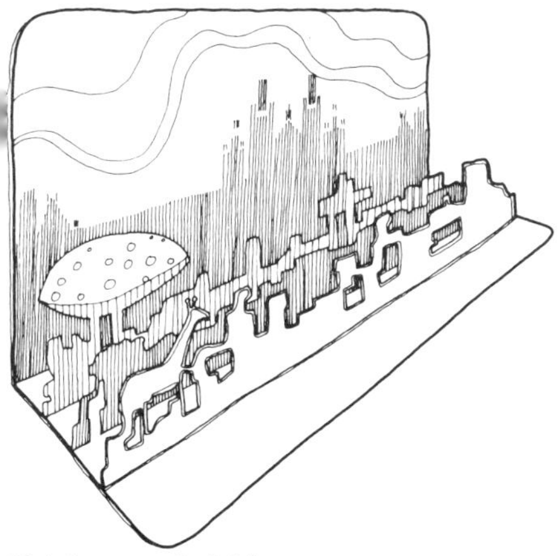

Kelvingrove kaleidoscope
Gallery Saturday Club, Glasgow Museums

A pop-up scene of the selected area made from cardboard and other simple materials, the construction represents the concept of a 'Kelvingrove kaleidoscope' as imagined by the children of the museum club. The proposal involves a host of novel and original ideas, some practical, some almost bizarre! Prehistoric monsters, Celtic crosses, telescopes and railway locomotives appear as cardboard cut-outs against a background of a facade of the galleries. Sound effects—animal noises, etc.—need to be imagined in the ear of the beholder!

Museum Saturday Club. The group presenting this proposal consists of eight schoolchildren all aged 11 years.

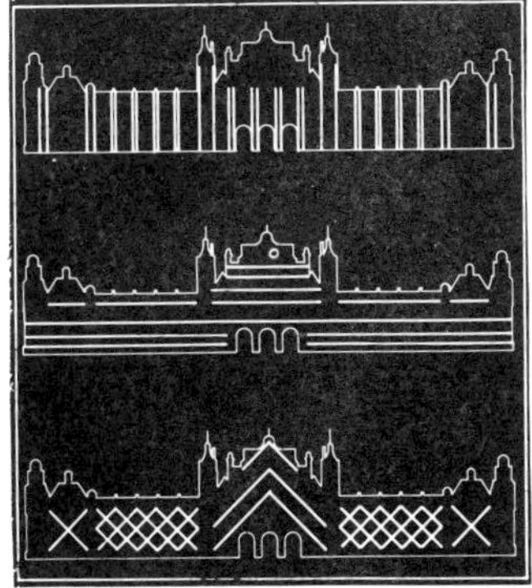

Light lines
Tom Heneghan, Mark Walker, Richard Woollard

The purpose of this proposal to generate a more widely held realisation of the qualities of good architecture. The museum building itself becomes the exhibit. During the evening the front elevation would be illuminated by a 5-minute programmed slide sequence which, visible from the gardens, would draw the public's attention to the finer points of the building's design— projected coloured light-lines illustrating its underlying proportional systems, its regulating lines and the interconnection of its major elements. The slide programme, which is educational, entertaining and picturesque would complement the building's daytime function as museum and art gallery.

Tom Heneghan born 1951 in London. Studied at the Architectural Association where he now lectures.

Mark Walker born 1951 in Hemel Hempstead. Studied at the Architectural Association. Works as architect.

Richard Woollard born 1949 in Weston super Mare. Studied at Cambridge. Works as architect.

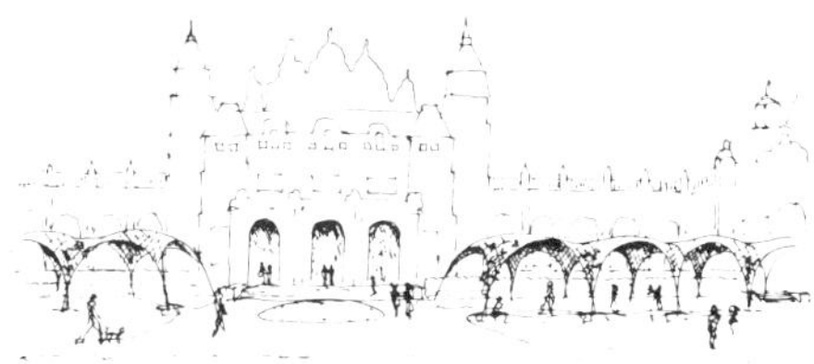

Kelvingrove promenade
William F Logan

The proposal is for an arbour with a new path system and benches to provide a sense of scale and enclosure to the now desolate area, while enhancing the feasibility of outdoor exhibitions. This new growing framework would be light and transparent, contrasting with the existing building while sympathising with its rhythmical quality. The supports for the arbour would be combination bench/planters, allowing it to be overgrown with colour while preventing vandalism. The path system would be modified to create a softer landscape before the severity of the main facade. The structure of the arbour is a grid shell of a elegant and technically innovative nature such as those developed by Frei Otto. Materials, assembly and erection would be inexpensive, simple, yet labour-intensive, allowing a large proportion of the funds to be recycled to the local community.

Born 1946 in Wilkes Barre PA, USA. Studied at Princeton and Harvard. Works as architect and designer.

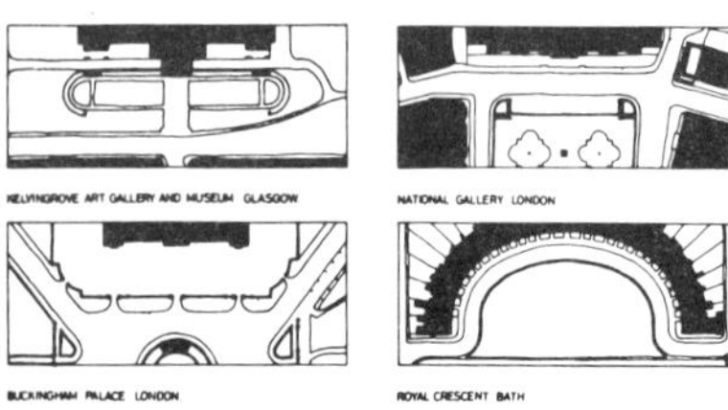

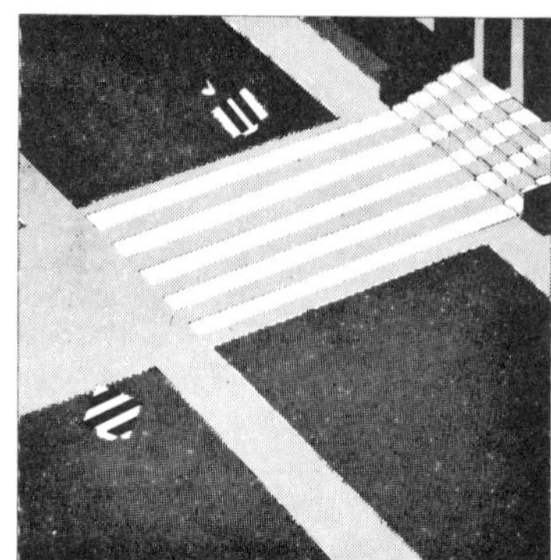

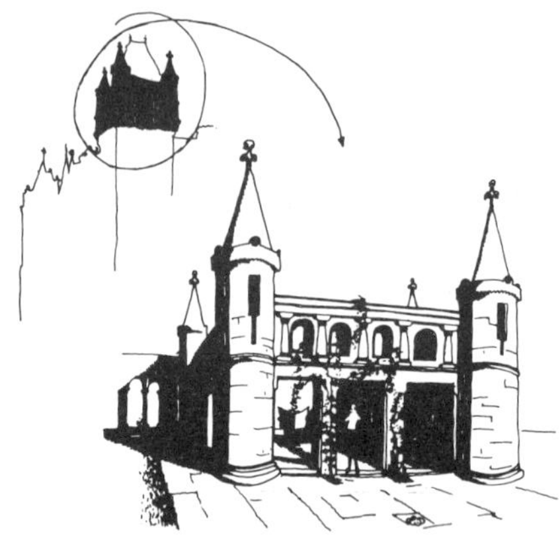

Kelvingrove promenade II
Justin de Syllas

The building appears to be smaller than it is. The terrace is bare and forbidding. My intention is to provide a more intimate and inviting scale within the terrace so that the visitor is not overwhelmed by the building. The main element is the massing of a large number of trees which define the space by filling it. Under the canopy of foliage the intimate scale is established. Here there is a promenade linking screened garden spaces which serve as 'places of enjoyment and relaxation'. The promenade is entered through a gate echoing the existing portico and indicating that the terrace is an extension of the art gallery. A large external foyer links Argyle Road and the building and contains a kiosk, telephone booths and external exhibits. To each side are subsidiary spaces including a rose garden, small amphitheatre and pavilions with seats.

Born in 1943 in Maidenhead. Studied at the Architectural Association. Teaches at Portsmouth Polytechnic and works as architect.

Stripes museum
Gerard Taylor

In my design I have tried to provide a basic 'all weather' area which could be used and manipulated by the gallery staff and public. A place for winter and summer rain and sun day and night . . . a place . . . for adults and children . . . a place . . . to discover, to learn, to talk, to eat . . . to enjoy . . .

Born 1955 in Bellshill, Lanarkshire. Studies product design at the Glasgow School of Art.

Amazing city
Anthony Vogt, John Doak

The idea is to extend the Art Gallery's custodian role by using the available site as a park to contain memories of the past glories of Glasgow's fruity, urban Victorian heritage in the form of walls, windows, doorways, special features, etc., taken from buildings under demolition. They might be re-used to form outdoor seating, arcades, etc., and joined together to form a mild maze. One does not know for certain which buildings will actually be demolished, and the enmity that usually surrounds such a process makes it dangerous to forecast—particularly if this should be used as a lever to get rid of buildings of quality.

Anthony Vogt born 1932 in London. Studied architecture at University College. Teaches at the Mackintosh School of Architecture, Glasgow.

John Doak born 1959. Studies at the Mackintosh School of Architecture, Glasgow.

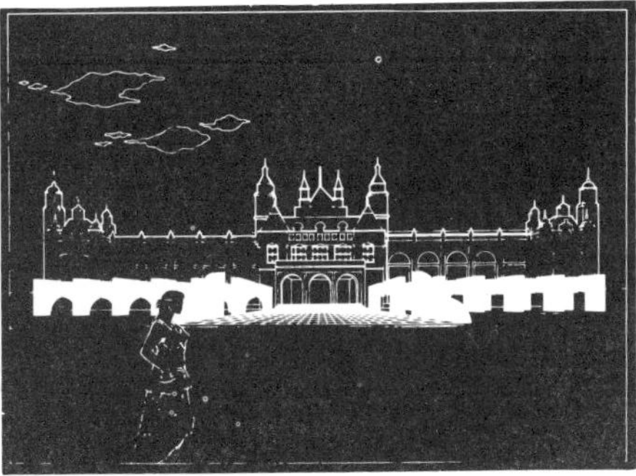

Twelve plus two
Ferry Zayadi

Twelve arches . . . twelve ivy-covered timber structures placed at regular intervals along the main axis of the terrace . . . a three-dimensional rhythmic modulation of the space in proportion with the scale and dimensions of the whole terrace and building . . . the ground surface to be paved with large stone slabs . . . the spaces between the arches may have seating and may also be used as display spaces which will then be perceived in succession as the visitor walks along. Facing the main entrance, on the left hand side, six arches with round openings; on the right hand side, six arches with square openings and, leading to the main entrance on each side, two undulant ivy-covered structures.

Born 1944. Studied Rome University Faculty of Architecture. Works as architect.

Finsbury Park Central

Design a focal point for a park

Finsbury Park is an area of 115 acres, and was opened in 1869; proposals have been accepted by the GLC for a gradual improvement (modernisation) programme to be carried out. The site in Finsbury Park proposed for some kind of feature or layout is, in fact, the highest part of this much used open space, being prominent in that respect, but also because it adjoins the popular boating lake. A recently built refreshment building forms one boundary of the area, which has some fine London planes and other trees flourishing in the area. The existing surface is tar-macadam.

The GLC Parks department will be happy to see proposals for any feature or layout which will be a focal point, or be of special interest in this area. There is an opportunity for an imaginative proposal and this would be welcomed by the Council. Competitors might like to consider that their proposal could be applied to many similar parks.

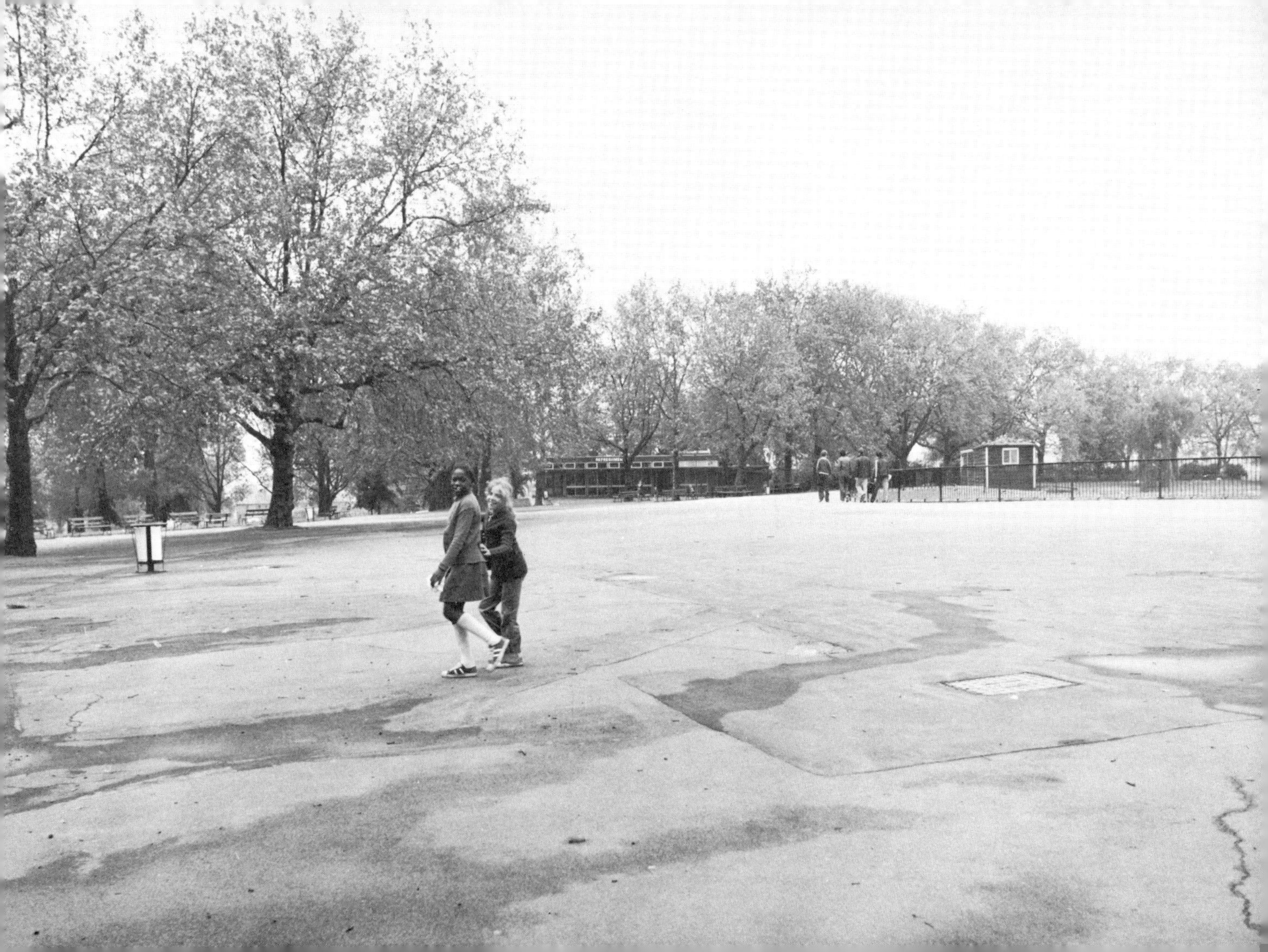

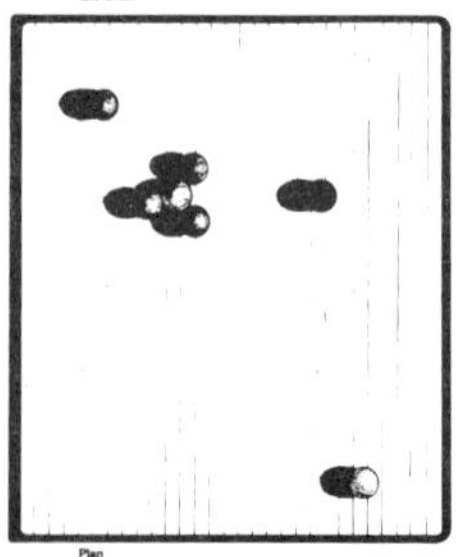

The snookered game
Alan Baron

My proposal is a large-scale set-piece which attempts to capture the colour, brilliance and precision of a game of snooker. I felt obliged to provide players of the game with a problem: a small matter of angles and trajectories; the position of the balls represents a snooker situation. Yellow is next to be played. With absolute control and precision an escape shot is playable. Not by myself however. I am attempting to provide a spectacle for the non-playing visitor. The dead flat, green table top set up with shiny coloured jewels— sorry, balls—is visually irresistible. It invites participation. The balls, 2m in diameter, would be cast in concrete with a car enamel type finish. The base would be a concrete platform with raised edge. The green baize would be 'astroturf'. Ideally the whole thing would be floodlit at night thus providing tantalising views from Seven Sisters Road.

Born 1941 in London. Studied graphic design at Hornsey College of Art. Works as graphic designer and studies interior design at Chelsea School of Art.

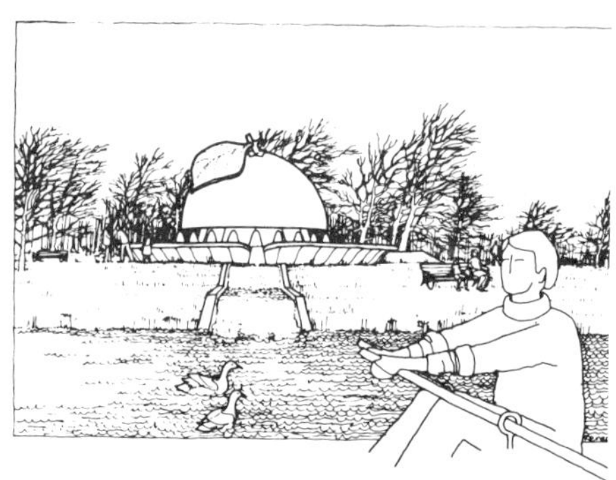

Orange squash lake
Meir Berk, Seving Berk

The problem: to provide a feature, a focal point in the area adjacent to the new café and to the boating lake in Finsbury Park. Our solution takes the form of a sculpture-fountain that will recycle some of the lake water to give the impression of an unlikely source for the existing boating lake. The sculpture is a glass-reinforced plastic orange which gently rotates on top of a squeezer. Water jets carefully located between the orange and the squeezer give the impression of the orange being squashed by an invisible hand. At night, the orange will be illuminated by using projectors placed under its shell, and the water jets will be picked up by lights placed behind them.

Meir Berk born 1945 in Tel-Aviv. Studied at State Academy of Fine Arts Department of Architecture, Istanbul and Thames Polytechnic. Works as architect.

Seving Berk born 1945 in Turkey. Studied at State Academy of Fine Arts Department of Architecture, Istanbul. Works as architectural designer.

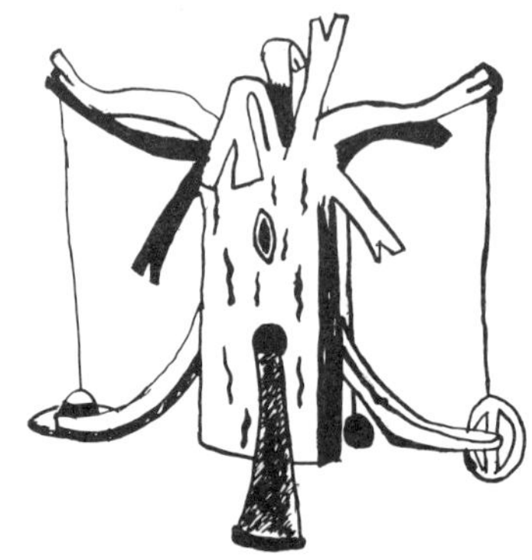

Tree of the future
Martyn Braine

My scheme is for a 12ft high tree of the future when real trees have perhaps died from pollution. It is hollow, 6 ft across, so that it can contain activities such as a helterskelter slide and climbing frame with bouncy rubber flooring for safety which could also be used for trampolining. The exterior has tentacles instead of branches and these could have ropes for swinging and there could also be a lookout tower. There is a window with special glass giving the same effect as a fly eye lens so that the viewer gets a distorted (futuristic) view of the surroundings. The tree will be made of concrete, with strong plastic tubing used for the helterskelter, wooden or metal rungs for the ladder (perhaps a very large precast concrete pipe could be modified to keep the cost down); rubber tyres, sprayed silver, could be used for the swings.

Born 1962. Attends Hyde Farm School, Balham.

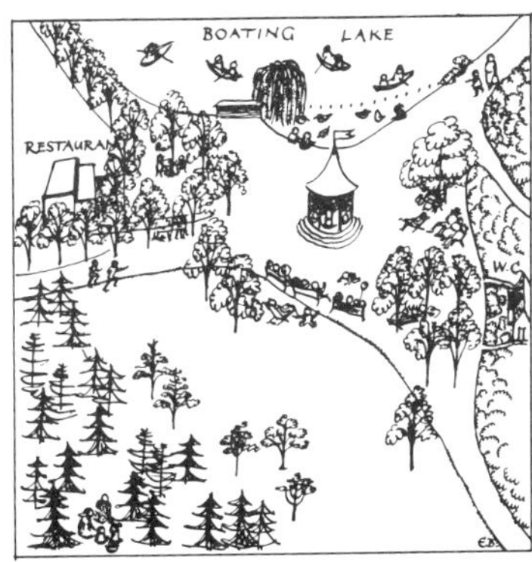

A focal point
Elizabeth Bulkeley

The site is bordered on 3 sides by a new restaurant, a boating lake and public conveniences. The fourth side is open and faces parkland with mature trees. The central area is large, empty and slopes away with a covering of dismal tarmac, plus a few fine trees. The whole area lacks unity and needs to be given a sense of being *somewhere*. As the hub of the area I propose a lively object such as a bandstand or a tough, simple sculpture of the kind that could be climbed over by children. Equally important measures to give the area a sense of intimacy would include planting a belt of conifirs to give protection from the prevailing wind, removing some of the lakeside railings to allow views across the lake and encourage children to feed the ducks, enlarging the sitting-out area in front of the restaurant and grassing-or gravelling-in redundant tarmac.

Born 1944 in Wolverhampton. Studied sculpture at the Royal Academy Schools. Now studies horticulture part-time.

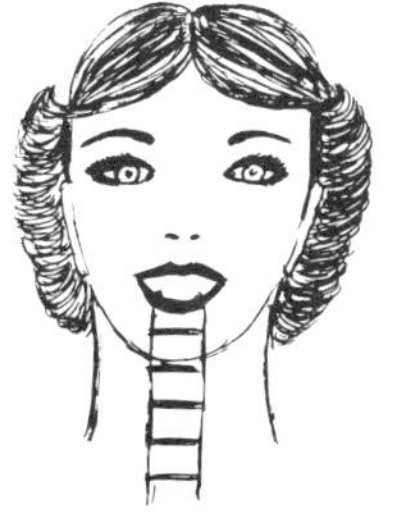
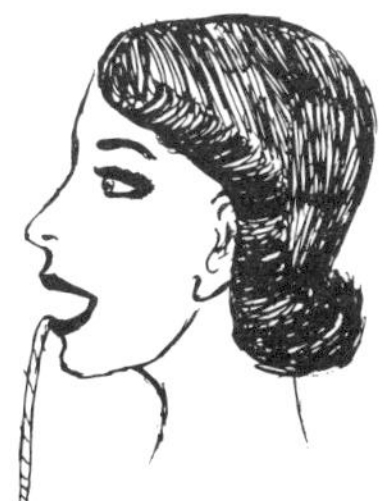

Head rest
Laura Bullard

The best way to describe the proposal is a giant head. You climb a small ladder, enter through the mouth and can sit inside the head. The eyes are windows which let in light and all over the inside of the head where the brain is are all the thoughts in the head. The head is a model of a lady's head and is made of fibreglass.

Born 1964 in Barnet. Attends Bishop Douglass School.

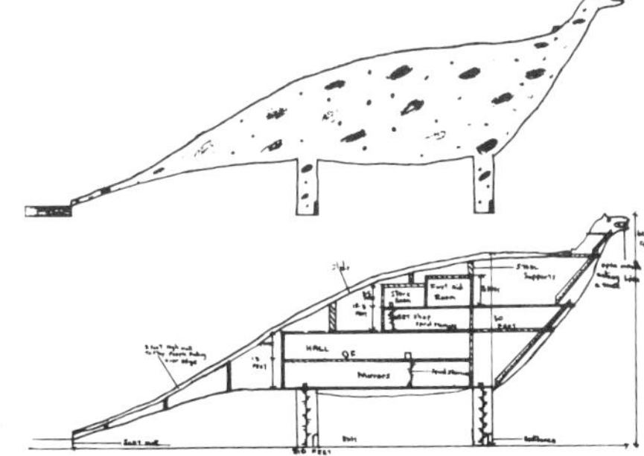

Monster
Adam Carter

The monster will be 62.5 feet tall and 210 feet long. Inside its body will be a sweet shop, hall of mirrors and a first aid room. To make your way up into the body you will have to go up spiral staircases and ordinary steps to make your way to the tower. The main structure will be made of steel and the covering of fibreglass or tough plastic. The monster will also have a 190 feet long slide on its back with 2 foot walls either side and a soft mat at the bottom of it measuring 10 feet long and 9 feet wide. *Born 1963. Attends Bishop Douglass School.*

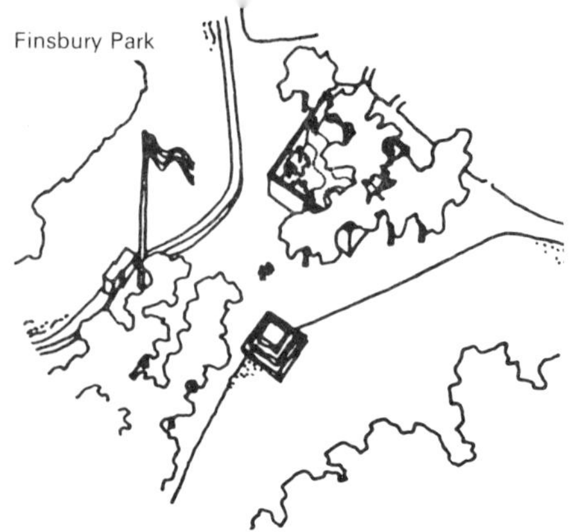

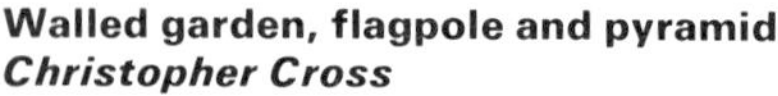

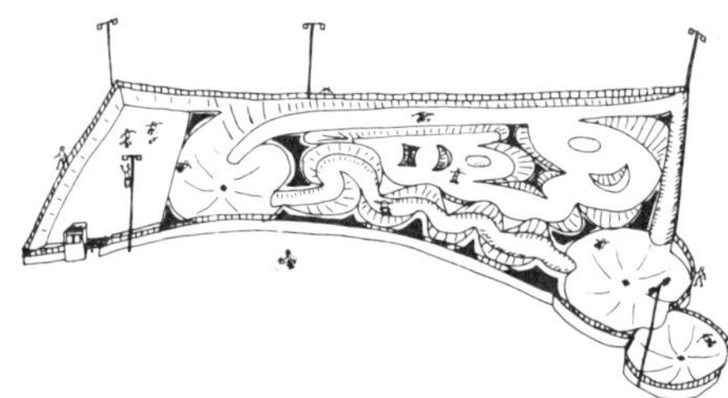

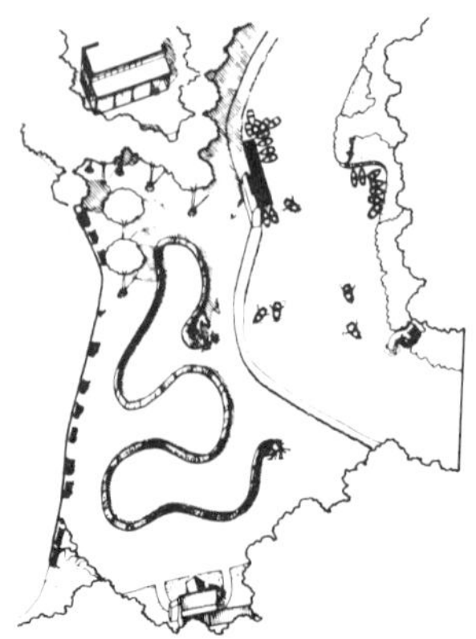

Walled garden, flagpole and pyramid
Christopher Cross

On first contact the park feels uneasy. Was it a guilty Victorian gesture to compensate for the failure to make a live city? It would be better if it was more urban with buildings lining its edges instead of trying to be like a dream of countryside. There is an irresistible draw to the top of the hill and the surprise of the lake, but when you get there the island in the centre destroys the magic. You are left in the windswept space below the café, the competition site. This proposal attempts to break down the bareness of the tarmac, provide contrasts and celebrate the trees with the aid of a flagpole, pyramid and walled garden. The flagpole is tall, *above* the trees. From the edges of the park you can see flags flown in celebration (or just to say the café's open). The pyramid rises *into* the trees. Children climb on it; it's a place to sit, or a stage for speech or music. The walled garden encloses space *under* the trees; an oasis with fountain and exotic plants.

Born 1939. Studied at the Architectural Association, where he now works as well as in private practice.

Skate park
Adam Finch, Dominic Hepher

We propose to build a skateboard park which would consist of a series of bowls, banked slalom runs and a flat freestyle area to accommodate safely the growing number of skateboarders in the Greater London area. It would be made from cement and so safety equipment would be essential and compulsory and a hire shop would be situated by the entrance. A skatepark is dearly needed and long overdue. Skateboarders have been banned from most parks and from the birthplace of the London skateboard— the Kensington Broadwalk. In America 12 skateboarders were killed on the road before a skatepark was built. So far in London there have been no deaths but some people say that there will have to be at least one before the necessity to build a skatepark is realised.

Adam Finch born 1961 in London. Attends Pimlico Comprehensive and studies animation at the Central School of Art part-time.

Dominic Hepher born 1963 in London. Attends Alleyns School, Dulwich.

Serpent
Henry Hagger, Michael Wright

Aim: to use ingredients of humour, colour and fantasy to bring life and enjoyment to this featureless area. Proposal: a serpent slides from his secret island lair into the murky depths of the lake and reappears with great force bursting through the tarmac promenade. It winds its way towards the pavilion before turning and raising its head to keep a watchful eye on the children in their boats. Material: 1. Prefabricated sections. (i) pre-cast concrete decorated by children with mosaic or a pigmented membrane. (ii) GRP—a coloured transparent membrane over a GRP skin pumped with expanded polystyrene foam for rigidity. 2. In-situ construction: Gunite—armature built on site sprayed and surfaced as pre-cast concrete sections.

Henry Hagger born 1946 in London. Studied architecture at Newcastle University. Works as architect.

Michael Wright born 1946 in Leicester. Studied at Newcastle Polytechnic. Works as sculptor at Madame Tussaud's.

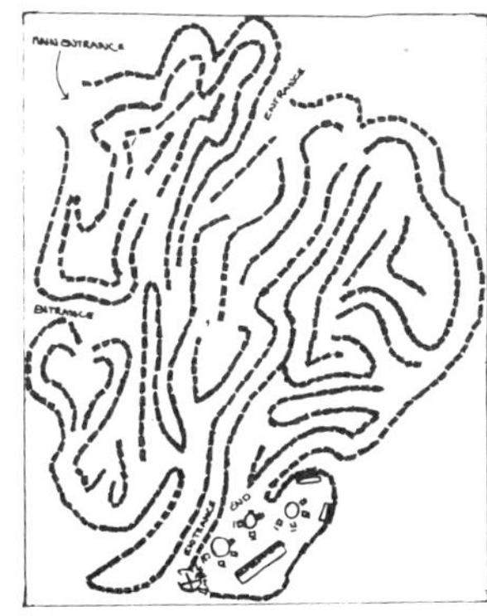

Maze
Jacqueline Hurley

My entry is a new kind of maze to go in the open space at Finsbury Park. My maze is different because it has no hedges or solid walls, but just tall tapering pillars of concrete with small, but not too small gaps in between them. Each pillar would be 9' to 10' high so that they would be hard to climb over. The purpose of the gaps is so that you can see through to the path you are aiming for but cannot get to it. This would be off-putting because you would immediately go to where you can see the path (one hopes) but not to where the opening of the path is. Another thing that will be confusing is that the whole maze is to be painted jazzy colours, which will be hard for the eyes to cope with especially when you can see several lines of pillars at one time. This is my theory of how the maze will work; I am not a scientist so I can't say for certain how people will react to jazzy colours and concrete pillars, but just in case my maze does get built I hope that I am right.

Born 1963 in London. Attends Bishops Douglass School.

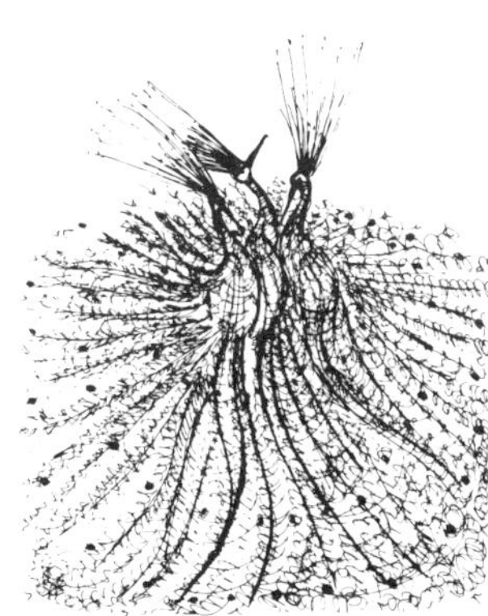

Peacocks in the park
Ruth Lakofski

This is a wan, desolate park, a poet's park. It has many amenities but nothing old or beautiful. Amongst the trees I suggest this peacock mosaic sculpture. The surface of the given site is a misty blue tarmac out of which the mosaic rises, its edges merging and extending into it. Irridescent glass mosaic pieces are chosen to give an 'ancient' feeling as if it had been there forever. The tempestuous birds, swirling up out of a sea of feathers, stand about 8 to 10 ft high and have a frosted finish merging with the spread of the tails. The sculpture has been designed to gain from all weathers and times of day: the pouring rain, dull grey skies, sunshine or moonlight. In a thunderstorm it should add magic to the park. Natural weathering is taken into account so that age will add to its beauty.

Born in the mid-'30s in Africa. Studied art and architecture and continues to work in the byways of both.

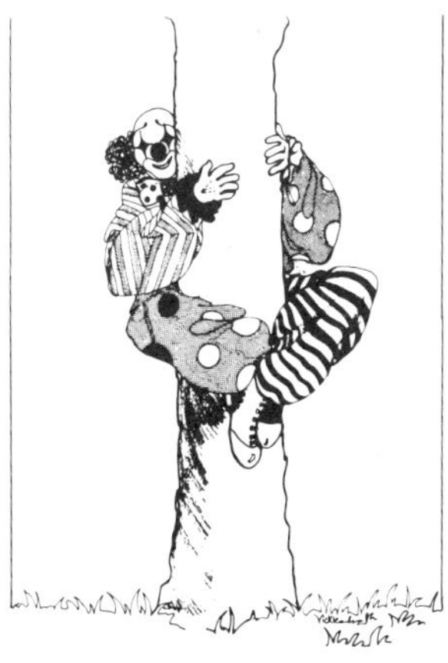

Bring in the clowns
Vicki MacKenzie

I am primarily trying to achieve the atmosphere of this park when the circus comes round. This means there are a lot more cheerful colours making this park what it should be throughout the year and not only when the circus comes. My solution is a few clowns hiding, climbing, within the trees in the specified area. Additionally they could be made detachable, allowing them to rotate once a year around the park. Perhaps the detail could be 3-dimensional so that children could also participate with the sculpture.

Born in 1955 in Portland, Oregon, USA. Studies furniture design at Middlesex Polytechnic.

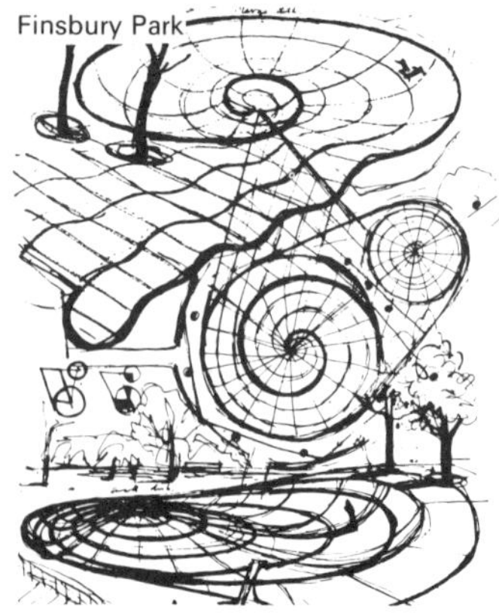

Skateboard park
Lawrence Preece

I wanted a scheme that had a function but allowed for sculptural and architectural invention. The site is depressing in its apparent disregard for the comfort of the many people who use it; the vast area of tarmac and the seating bear no relationship to anything; the whole area is visually and physically unpleasant. A skateboard park seemed to satisfy my requirements and fulfil a need. The design is generated from the existing trees, pays no heed to the tarmac and is developed from the two longest uninterrupted lengths possible, terminated by circular areas of differing dimensions. I then devised a scheme whereby all surfaces might be continuous from the skaters' point of view and allowed for a great deal of invention. It was important that it should not be an eyesore, that the present use be taken into consideration and that skateboarders should not use any other areas.

Born 1942 in Shepton Mallet. Studied ceramics at Brighton College of Art. Teaches part-time at Middlesex Polytechnic and Chelsea School of Art.

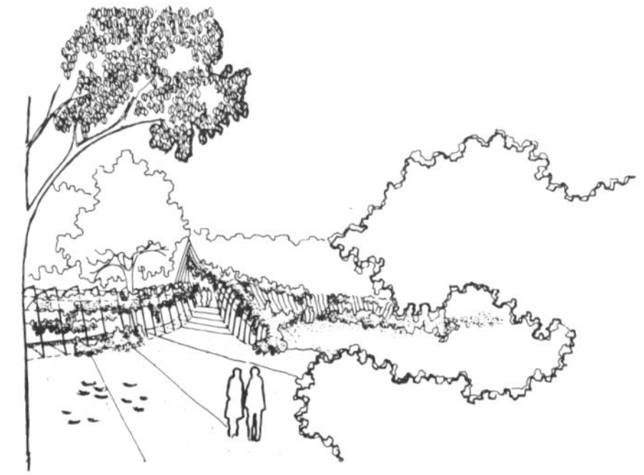

Hollow mound
Mike Richardson, Jorge Toro

From a distance the form emphasises the hillside site and establishes a central point of interest in the park. Approaching the site the spatial qualities of the tree-lined avenues extend inside the sculptured forms. Once inside, an open textured structure defines an interlocking system of spaces without enclosing them and orientates attention towards particular activities or views characteristic to the site. The process of establishing 'place' is continuous. The forms as presented are not compromised by anticipating social and creative activities, but should fairs, open air theatre, or music or exhibitions develop, the scheme extends naturally to encompass them.

Mike Richardson born 1945 in Carlisle. Studied architecture at the Northern Polytechnic and urban design at Manchester University.

Jorge Toro born 1945 in Columbia. Studied architecture at National University of Columbia. Both work as architects.

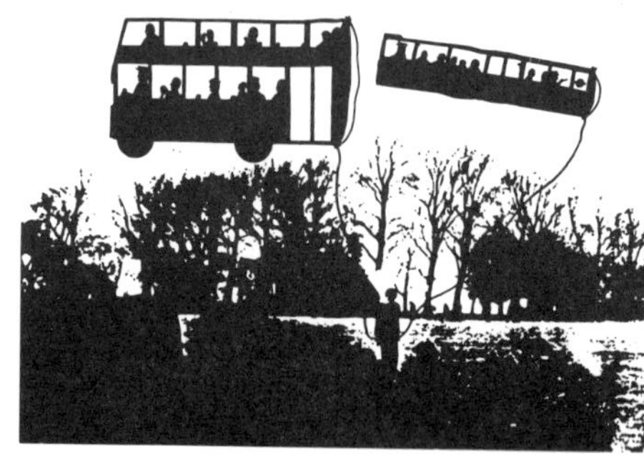

Finsbury follies
3rd year, St Marylebone Grammar School

These ideas developed from making and flying kites in the park. It was a very windy day and so it was decided to design something which would utilise the idea of wind and movement. As the site was on a hill surrounded by trees, it would not be seen in the summer when the trees were in leaf. This would mean designing something in an enclosed space near ground level, or something above the trees which would be seen from a long distance and could be lit at night.

'We chose things which would change shape and direction in the wind as the landscape does'. *G Howes.*

'It seemed to be a place where there was a constant flow of wind and since we had both height and wind we thought it would be nice to make moving objects which would be more eye-catching'. *S Kanagasabai.*

'We had to make the object move because otherwise it would have been like all other monuments: still and boring'. *V Robinson.*

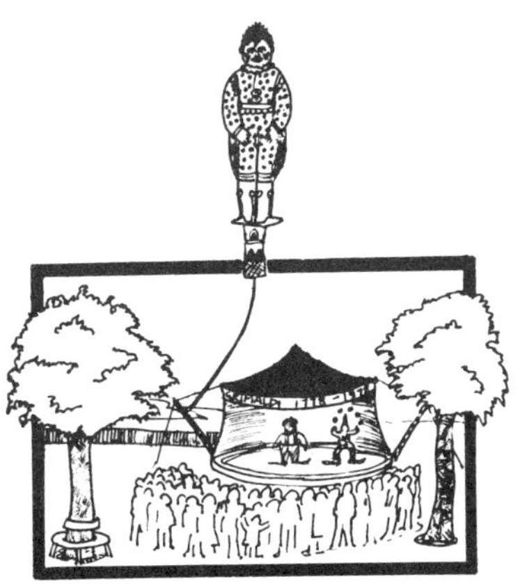

Grimaldi's bicentennial
E A Stevens

Joseph Grimaldi—the father of clowning—was born in London in 1778. Apart from a gravestone in an Islington cemetary he has no memorial. My proposal involves a giant hot-air balloon in the shape of Grimaldi (like the Robertsons' Golly balloon) suspended high above the competition site. The colourful balloon would be visible from miles around and would attract people back to the park. Beneath the balloon, in the shade of the trees, would be a small covered arena. Displays of clowning could be staged here as part of the celebrations commemorating Grimaldi's birth. Colour and vitality would return to the drab site.

Born 1952 in Redruth, Cornwall. Studied physics and works as journalist.

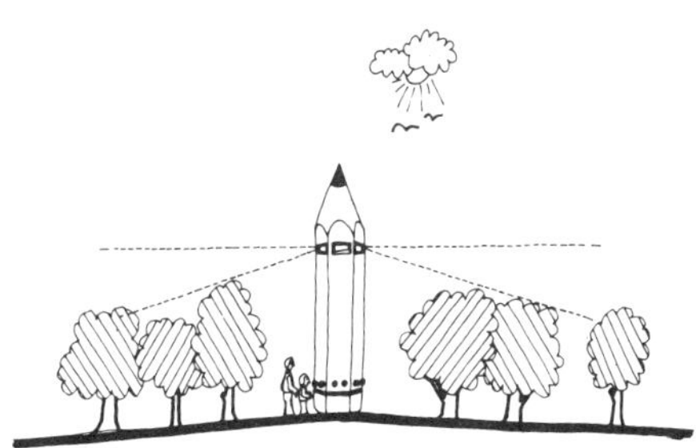

Pointed observations
William Thuburn

The design is a hexagonal periscope on a light steel frame enabling spectactors to enjoy six different aerial views; it grew out of the following considerations:
as the site is already an attractive space the feature should not occupy too much land; it should encourage people to have an active relationship with it, which suggests some form of machine, instrument or toy; the site, although elevated, is sheltered by trees, which makes the possibility of looking above them an attractive one; the device encourages and facilitates an interest in the remainder of the park and in the surrounding borough.
Variations could include adjustable mirrors to permit scanning in a vertical plane and a version which rotates around a central column.

Born 1942 in Alexandria, Scotland. Studied urban sociology in Chicago and regional studies at the London School of Economics. Works as adviser on development problems in the Third World. Interested in de-mystifying environmental planning.

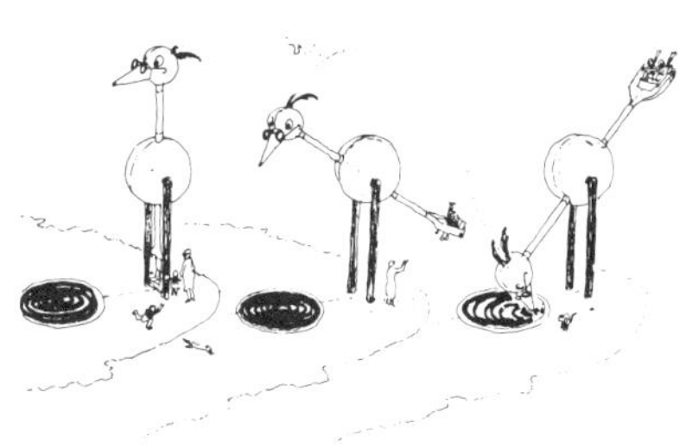

Finsbury stork
David Walker

This project is for children and the child in every adult. It is a 30ft high stork, made of brightly coloured plastic and steel, working by capillary action. It is sited next to the lake with its own pond, and will give rides to well-harnessed infants.

Born in 1940 in Tredegar, South Wales. Studied at RWA School of Architecture, Bristol and University of Bristol. Teaches architecture at Gloucestershire College of Art and Design.

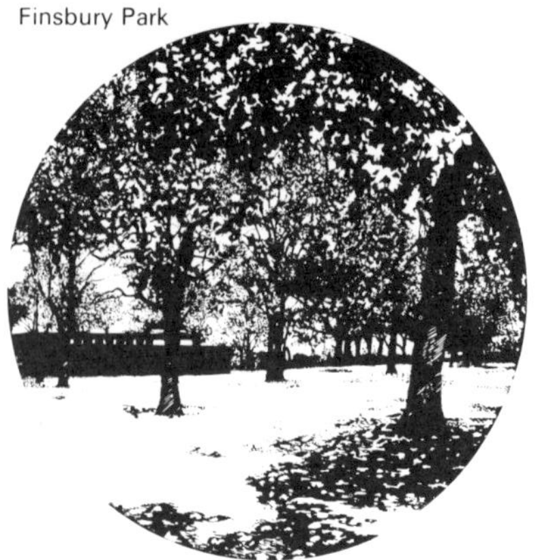

Stuff the genius loci?
Derek Walker Associates

With a responsible attitude to the limited budget we questioned the brief. Would the provision of an additional structural focal point represent the best value for money? We felt that an attempt to upgrade the existing facilities would improve the amenities of the site and perhaps form a blueprint for future work in the park and hopefully other similar parks. The operations and improvements chosen as being most valuable are: tree surgery and a planting policy ensuring replacement and maintenance on a seasonal cycle; tree grids commemorative of Jubilee Year; resurfacing of the immediate area; replacement benches and waste bins. Assuming a surplus of money, a list of additional facilities has been prepared. They cover a wide range of possibilities and functions and any one or more of these would help generate a greater amenity value for the site. *Architectural practice.*

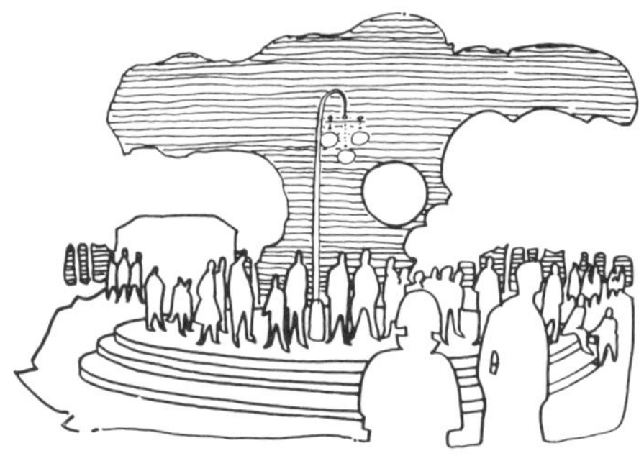

Nearly new clothes exchange
Denis R Wilkinson

It's like a stage set, a raised platform filled with cut-out figures of people, painted, waiting for chalk artwork— eyes, nose, mouth, face, neck, etc. Onto these cut-outs are placed old clothes either for sale, exchange/barter or give-away. We get a mingling of the living and the fixed—with all kinds of comings and goings—all set under the old pawnbrokers' sign—three brass balls. The gathering could be a regular summer Sunday morning affair, maybe like a big fancy-dress-do. During the off-peak weekdays, the cut-outs become a permanent gathering place—a magnificent set of bird/pidgeon perches—set under the symbol of the brokers' balls. From the distance the set will look like the silhouette of lots of people gathered together. Add lights, a speaker-system and it could turn into a choir, a stage show or setting for impromptu theatre and busking.

Born in Sunderland. Studied at the University of Durham and University of Pennsylvania. Works as landscape architect.

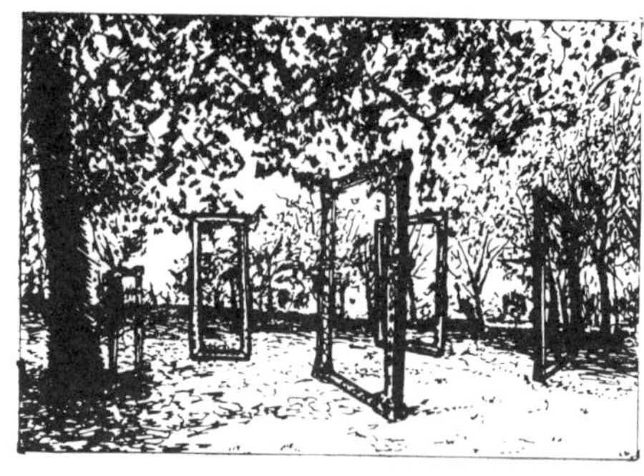

Open air gallery in Finsbury Park
Trevor Williamson

In my opinion parks are for the people who visit them. This design is intended for people to be able to participate in some way. The group of frames in the park form an open air gallery, each of the nine frames being a replica of one found in a real gallery. Pictures normally have real frames framing artificial landscapes, but here there are artificial frames framing real landscapes. The view contained within the frame will be continually changing because of constantly moving people. The frames would be of varying sizes so that even a small child could relate to one of them. They would also be strong enough for children to swing or climb on them if they wanted to do so.

Born 1956 in Birmingham. Studies interior design and related studies at Trent Polytechnic.

Lambeth Walk cover-up

Ideas for hoardings for redevelopment sites

Many areas of the inner city and town centres appear forgotten as part of the desolate scene of sites waiting to be redeveloped: the result of the bulldozer flattening obsolete buildings long before redevelopment takes place and corrugated iron sheeting sealing off the site becoming rusty and unsightly. These areas could be greatly improved by some imaginative yet still practical form of site boundary fencing.

The aim of this section of the competition is to search for a better design for hoardings which could be widely used but will hopefully be implemented on one particular site in central London within the Lambeth Walk Comprehensive Development Area. Details and requirements of the Lambeth Walk Comprehensive Development Area site are given but it is hoped that the design solution could be used generally for similar sites.

Lambeth Walk is one of London's most famous street markets but the crowded market that inspired Lupino Lane's popular "Doing the Lambeth Walk" song, is now one of South London's most modern local shopping centres, having been redeveloped as part of the GLC's Lambeth Walk Comprehensive Development Area. The southern end of the shopping street remains in a semi-derelict state. This part is now to be rebuilt and while this is going on it is important to maintain an attractive approach to the new shopping precinct. The objective is therefore to design a hoarding that will prove an effective safety barrier against the rebuilding works while creating a pleasant and attractive temporary approach to the new shops.

Location

The redevelopment site is situated in the south-west corner of the Lambeth Walk C.D. It lies between Black Prince Road and the new shopping precinct.

Originally more shops were proposed at this end of Lambeth Walk, with housing above as the extension to the new shopping precinct. It is now thought that the shops already built will be enough to meet local demand. The area will now be redeveloped with housing and community facilities.

Objectives of the Competition

1. To design an attractive and strong form of hoarding.
2. To create an attractive walkway to the shopping precinct during redevelopment.

Requirements for the Hoardings

1. The walkway may well have to be realigned during the course of construction so the hoardings must be able to be resited.
2. The walkway must be well lit.
3. The hoarding must be a minimum height of 2.13 metres (7 feet) and the walkway not less than 2.74 metres wide (9 feet).
4. It would be desirable to allow people to see into the building site at selected points.
5. Advertising panels may be introduced into the design of the hoardings.
6. While the exact alignment of the walkway can not be fixed yet, it can be assumed for the purpose of the competition that it would be approximately 100 metres long.
7. The hoarding will be needed for 2 to 3 years. However, obvious advantages would be ease of construction and a design which allowed for re-use of the hoarding on another site awaiting redevelopment.
8. Competitors may choose to use alternatives to the customary plywood or corrugated steel hoarding. However, another approach would be to suggest a different way of treating standard hoardings.

Implementation

The redevelopment site is due to be completely cleared by December 1978, allowing rebuilding to start by May 1979. The hoarding may have to be erected in stages, as and when properties are acquired and demolished. The competition winner therefore must be able to ensure availability of his or her design for implementation by December 1977, one year before the site has to be completely cleared. The exact alignment of the walkway can not be fixed until the detailed plans of the redevelopment have been completed and approved. Competitors are advised that the current cost of hoarding in high quality plywood is approximately £14 per metre at October 1976 prices. If the winning design is to be adopted for wider use it should be capable of being manufactured at a comparable price.

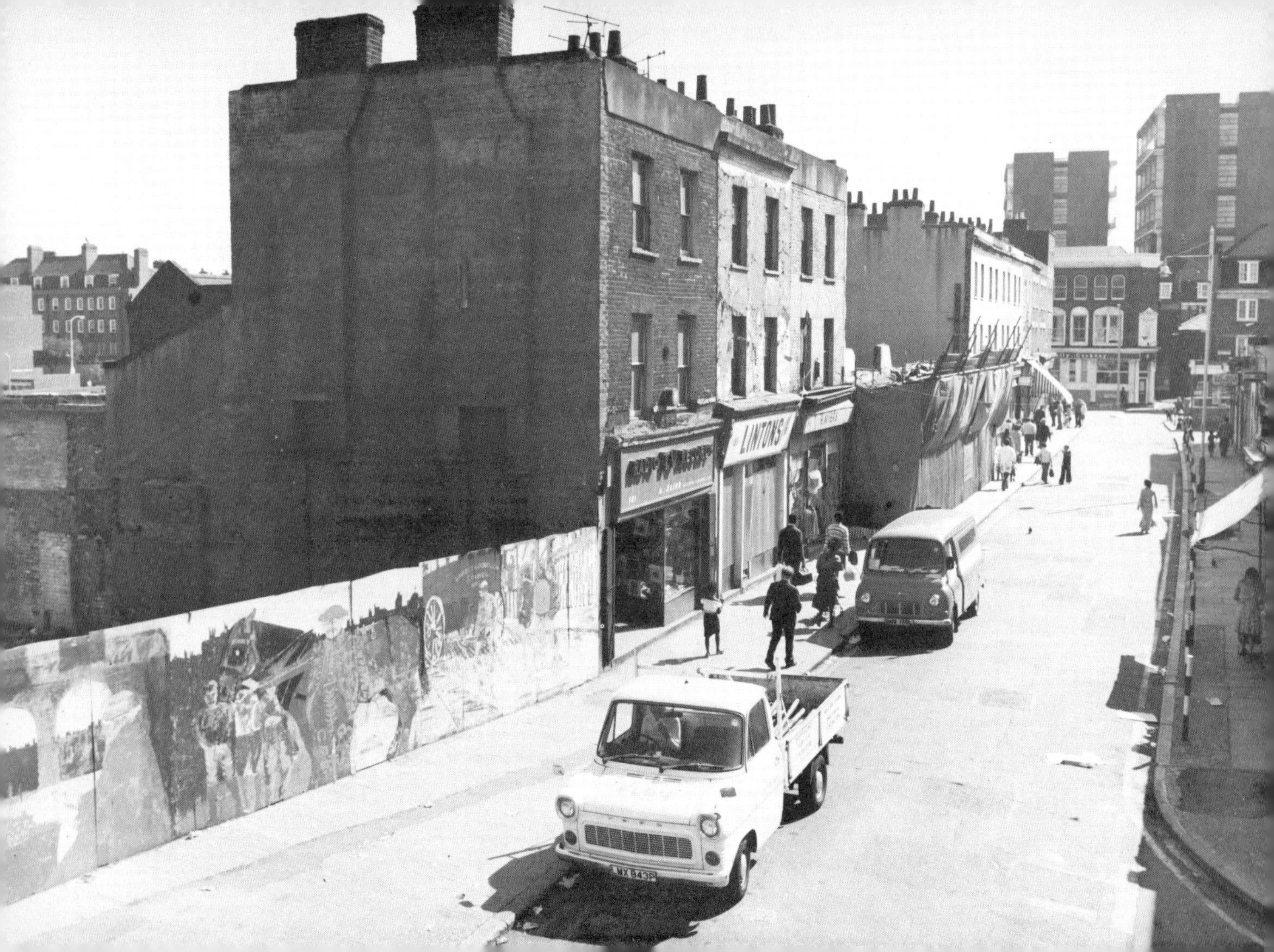

LINTONS

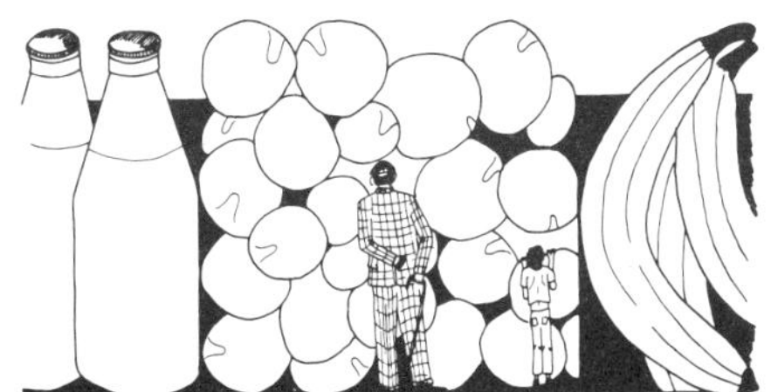

Tasty hoarding
Michael Bell

Walking by hoardings generally the only noticeable features are any posters that might be stuck to them, and the tendency is to walk past these blank walls as quickly as possible. I have tried to break up this featureless barrier to provide a colourful display that gives an illusion of varying depths as well as breaking the flat outline of normal hoardings. Basic traditional household items and goods form the basis of the designs, readily identifiable by local inhabitants and suitable in an urban shopping district; the theme gives a unity along a length of hoarding and is easily dismantled and rearranged differently. Mock-ups of products could be incorporated, or selected advertisers might be pleased to acquire a site on which to place a giant replica of their product in part of a scheme to brighten the environment.

Born 1952 in Teddington, Middlesex. Studies landscape architecture at Thames Polytechnic.

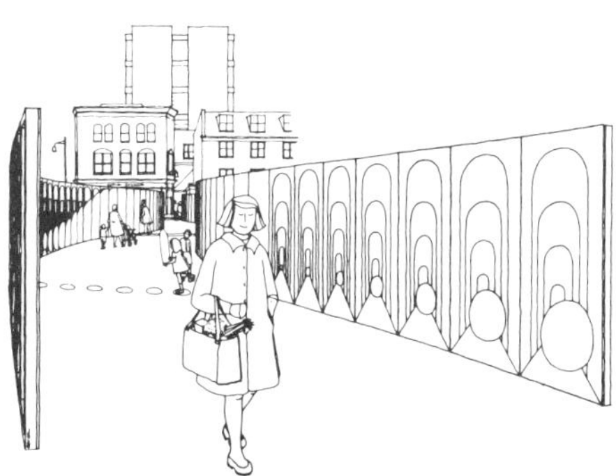

The elusive green ball
Meir Berk

The problem: to devise a hoarding system which is cheap, flexible and is so designed as to serve as a model for wider application than the Lambeth Walk site. The solution: the interpretation of the 'time' element involved in experiencing a walkway, coupled with the repetition created by a succession of modular units, manifests itself here as a cartoon-like 'sequence'. A green ball seems to rush along fictitious corridors situated on both sides of the curved walkway, crossing the road in two places which separate each sequence. The use of standard modular plywood units, pre-sprayed using a set of templates prepared by the artist, provides a cheap and infinitely flexible solution in which various designs can be developed using the same basic principle.

Born 1945 in Tel-Aviv. Studied at the State Academy of Fine Arts Department of Architecture, Istanbul and Thames Polytechnic. Works as architect.

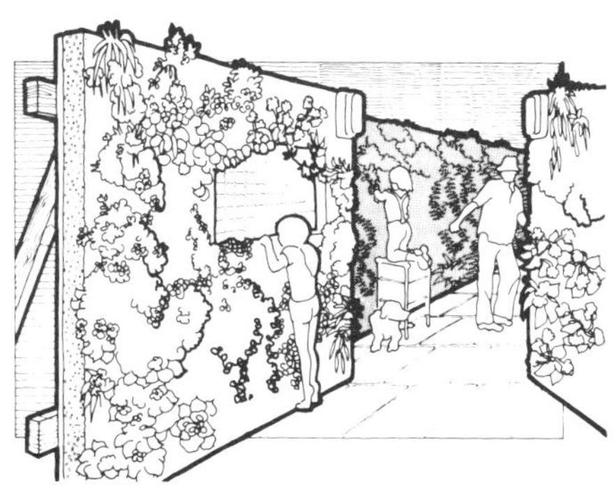

Garden fence
Adrian Corry, David Edgerley, Neil Taylor

By growing suitable plants on the specially treated vertical face of the site-hoarding, life, colour and vitality can be introduced into a previously neglected space. The design minimises the need for care and maintenance, the responsibility for which could in some way be given to the community, possibly to children from a local school.

Adrian Corry born 1949 in Moascar, Egypt. David Edgerley born 1949 in London. Neil Taylor born 1949 in Portsmouth. Post-graduate industrial design students at the Royal College of Art.

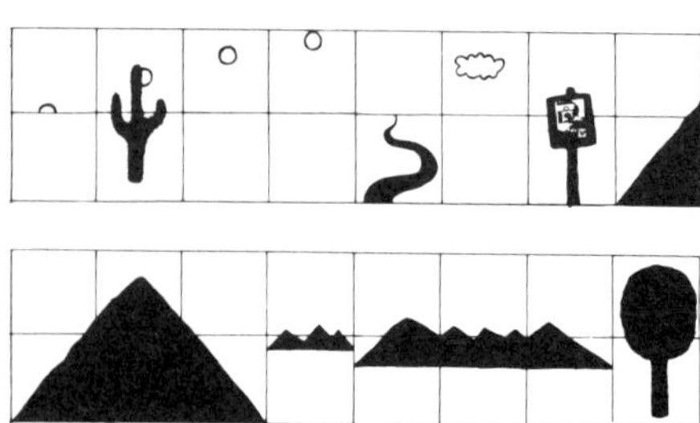

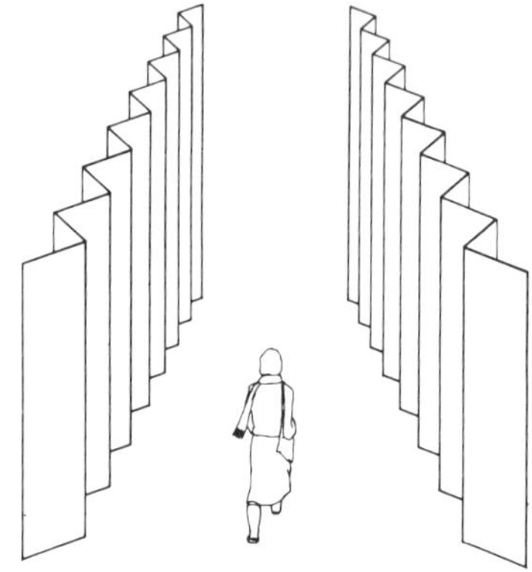

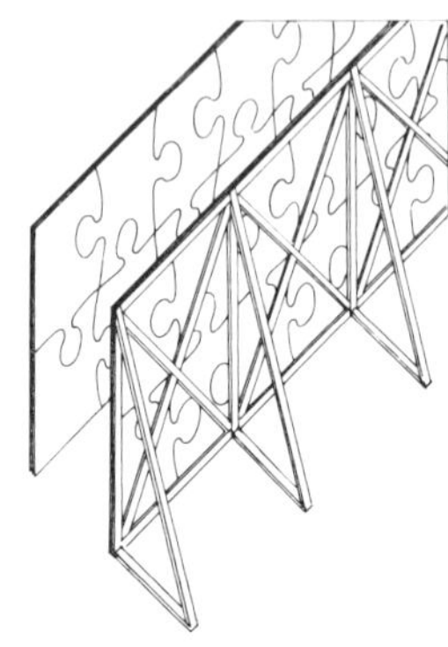

Endless journey
Charles Garrad

A design of a number of compatible pictorial elements to be stencilled onto 8ft × 4ft plywood sheets and used as a hoarding to provide colour, movement, interest and a sense of space. They can be erected in different combinations forming an endless and everchanging landscape. Either large background images are sprayed through stencils in a workshop and smaller details added using handheld stencils once the hoarding has been erected, or the whole picture can be planned for each individual site using a model before the spraying takes place. In either case it is possible for the people living in the locality and/or those constructing the fence to have a say in the final result. In mass production the colours can be changed as paint runs out, thus moving easily through grassland, desert, sea, day, night, using the same stencils. The possibilities are almost limitless!

Born 1952 in Somerset. Studied at Stourbridge, and Cardiff and Chelsea Schools of Art. Works as artist and part-time lecturer at various art colleges.

Lambeth steps
Tom Heneghan, Mark Walker, Richard Woollard

This proposal is not specific to Lambeth Walk although there is the possibility of developing the scheme with closer links with the neighbourhood. 8ft × 2ft sheets of plywood are erected in a corrugated plan form—the extra area of plywood compared to ordinary hoarding is offset by a significant reduction in framework—the corrugated plan form being structurally stable. The lack of framework permits simple construction and easy realignment. The corrugated plan form has been used because two different paintings may be mixed on alternate panels of the wall and occupy the same space, but be viewed separately depending on the passer-by's direction of movement. Local schools may be invited to prepare these paintings. This should create a local identity as well as a degree of self-policing.
For biographical notes see catalogue number 65.

Lambeth Walk hoarding
Gillian Hinds

The hoarding consists of interlocking interchangeable jigsaw pieces held vertically by a supporting structure from behind. The hoarding may be left unadorned or painted either by the community or by an artist. As the pieces are interchangeable, subsequent reconstruction may result in different alignments causing unexpected combinations.

Born 1947 in London. Studied painting at Chelsea School of Art and sculpture at the Royal College of Art. Works as artist and tutor for the Open University art and environment course.

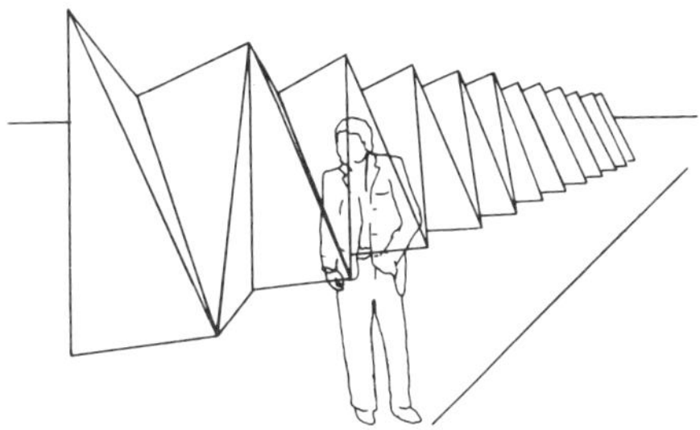

Flexible articulated hoardings
Dave Lovett

To provide a hoarding system which is strong, stable and flexible, yet of visual interest. This system can be expanded and contracted lengthwise and will allow realignment; modules can be simply inserted or removed without impairing stability or visual effect. Contraction, expansion and alignment is effected by a series of hinges along each edge, every alternate set being of the 'drop' variety allowing for the removal of two flaps; with this arrangement of hinges any shape of alignment can be made. The panels can have viewing ports easily let into them. Storage is made easy by each module of two flaps folding flat. The surfaces can be dyed or stained and coated in a clear polyurethane paint.

Born 1950 in London. Worked as a theatre design technician and lighting designer. Now studies mural design at Chelsea School of Art.

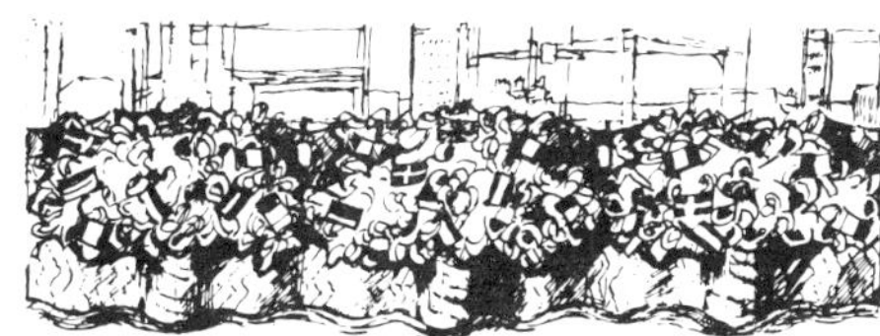

Jubilee trees
Morley College Soft Sculpture Group

Discarded fertilizer bags and sacking are cut into strips and woven and knotted through wire mesh to make durable artificial trees, which compensate for the lack of natural vegetation. The mesh is selected to suit different types of hoarding, bent or laid against a fence or supported by scaffolding. A height of 7 to 8 ft was chosen as relating better to the human scale than the huge tower blocks nearby, and viewing gaps are made in the mesh to suit spectators of varying heights. Implementation is seen as a community project and could be carried out by schools. We would like to think that this involvement would make people more interested in their surroundings. Extra decoration for the trees is painted or stuck onto the plastic and could be changed frequently, ideas being based on local themes or events like Christmas or the Jubilee.

The Soft Sculpture Group is a non-vocational adult evening class in soft sculpture and three-dimensional design. Its students come from all walks of life and several live and work in Lambeth.

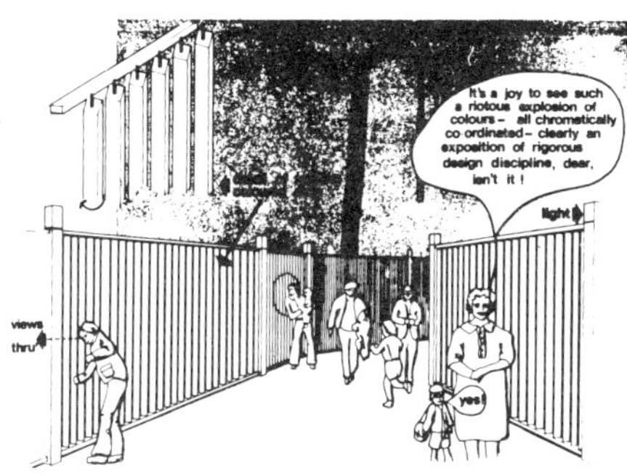

Revolving slat hoarding
Oakeley Turner Bate-Williams

The hoarding is constructed of component parts. The vertical square section slats are designed to rotate about a vertical axis. Each face of every slat is painted. The overall effect is that the colours of each slat combine with the colours on adjacent slats to produce myriad hues and patterns, which are perceived to change as the pedestrian passes by. The slats can be changed in position by the users, giving infinitely possible combinations of colours. This suggests many possibilities for subtle advertising.

Christopher Bate-Williams born 1949 in Cirencester. Studied at Gloucestershire College of Art & Design.

Gervase Oakley born 1950 in Herefordshire. Studied as above.

Jeremy Turner born 1948 in Brighton. Studied at Manchester University School of Architecture. All work as 'environmental troubleshooters, urban terra-ists and landscape architects. At present working in two private practices and in their own set-up in spare time.'

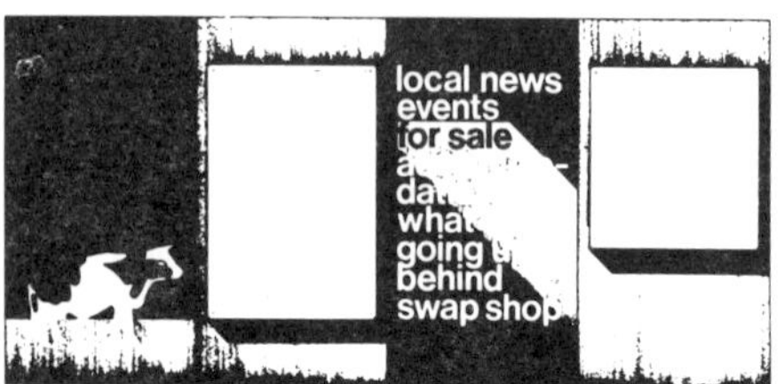

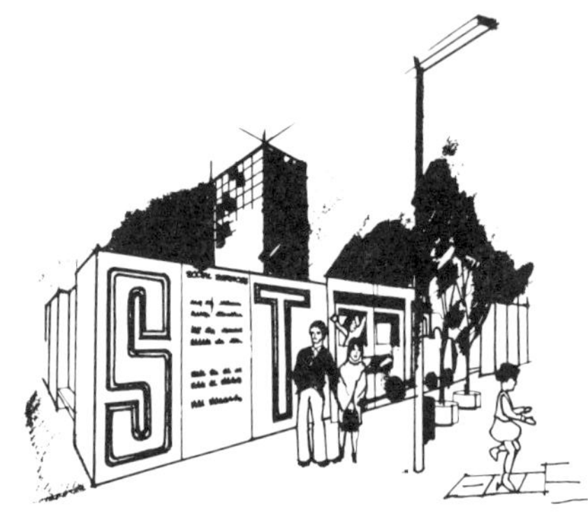

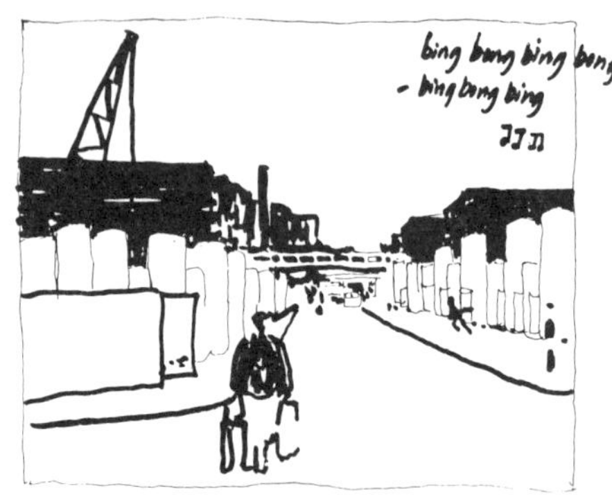

Rural scenes in Lambeth
Barrie Philip

The intention is to produce a series of panels that are visually interesting, and which encourage community participation by using conventionally constructed plywood panels, each of which has its own identity and function. By utilising a graphic treatment and a periodic change of height and form, it is proposed to provide an attractive and interesting walkway. The theme running through the panels is an easily identifiable rural scene of cows, trees, fields and flowers. The fundamental idea is that the hoarding should function as a community notice board, as well as giving information about what is going on behind the hoarding. The boards could be serviced by the local council who would be responsible for regularly updating the notices. The panels have been designed as independent units that can accommodate changes and be resited in any order.

Born 1949 in Dundee. Studied interior design at Glasgow College of Building. Works as exhibition systems designer.

A4B4
Andy Scott and John Harding

Hoardings contribute little to their environment. Their role has been to screen the activities behind them from the public gaze. However, they are actually large flat areas which provide potential for active social involvement. The proposal is for a series of bright colourful panels in either two- or three-dimensional form. The intention is to decorate them with strong, simple graphic imagery. This takes the form of an alphabet with pictures, or provides legal and social advice for a community. The decoration itself can be carried out very cheaply by known illustrators or even by local groups themselves. As a three-dimensional structure, the hoardings will provide the additional benefit of seating and play areas. A simple transformation from eyesore to community centre.

Andy Scott born 1949. Studied at Harrow School of Art. Works as exhibition, interior and graphic designer.

John Harding born 1955. Studies at the Architectural Association.

Musical fence
David Walker

This fence is made of panels in turn made from oil drums and corrugated iron. These panels are backed with resonating chambers on the Helmoltz principle. Each panel emits a discreet musical note and they would be tuned by a West Indian specialist consultant. The panels on one side of the street are for professional or experienced musicians, as they give a full range of notes in the harmonic scale—like a xylophone or vibraharp. On the other side of the street the panels are so arranged that their successive striking whilst walking past gives a rendition of 'Lambeth Walk—Ho'. This side of the street may be played by amateurs with a stick and strong legs. If the amateur side of the street is played in reverse it will produce a hitherto undiscovered melody called 'Oh—Klaw Htebmal'—an evocative noise of uncertain provenance.

Born in 1940 in Tredegar, South Wales. Studied at RWA School of Architecture, Bristol and University of Bristol. Teaches at Gloucestershire College of Art and Design.

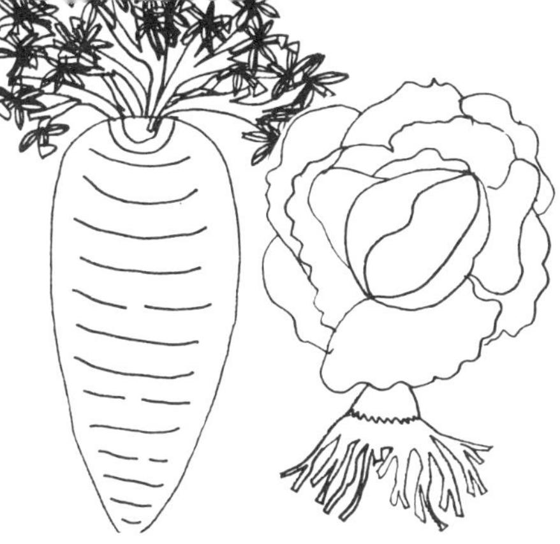

Vegetables in Britain
Susanna Williams

I thought that it would be nice for someone who was walking along the road to see something that was growing. Then I thought vegetables would be a good thing.

Born 1968 in London. Attends Thornhill Junior School, Islington.

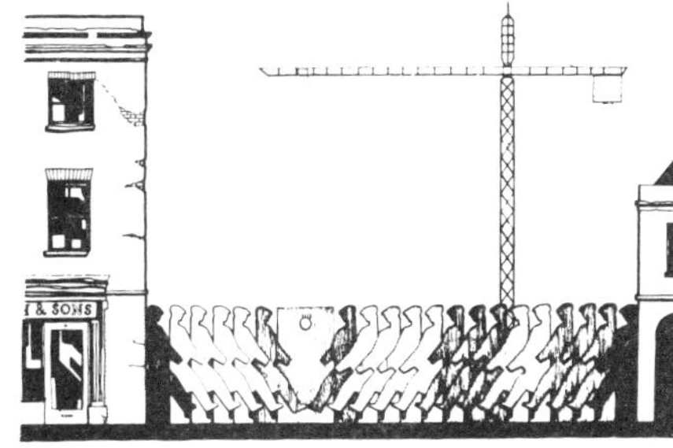

Lambeth walkers
Roy Winter

The proposal develops already tried and tested materials and methods into an exciting combination of symbolic characters. The overlapping figures suggest movement in a manner inspired by ancient Egyptian wall friezes and obviously, for this site, are suggestive of the *Lambeth Walk* and the Pearlies. Construction is very simple. A standard sheet of plywood or particle board is cut by jigsaw to form two figures, one being inverted. The figures are stained for longer life with colourful timber preservative solution. By screwing or nailing to a standard timber framework and by overlapping, interesting peep holes occur at various heights and the fretted silhouette sets up a rhythm of movement. The system may be re-used as required; different characters could be evolved for other sites. Solid panels can be introduced for advertising and provision made for lighting and even graffiti.

Born 1931 in Whitley Bay, Northumberland. Studied at Birmingham School of Architecture and Durham University. Works as landscape architect.

A window on the Thames

A new face for an old wharf at 125 Rotherhithe Street, Southwark, London

This Thames-side site is within London's old docklands and adjoins the St Mary's Rotherhithe Conservation Area. The intention has long been to open up this section of the river for use by both residents of and visitors to Rotherhithe and there is now the prospect of money becoming available to do this under the programme for environmental action in the Comprehensive Development Areas. The site affords extensive river views upstream to Tower Bridge and downstream to Limehouse.

The Conservation Area has a remarkable docklands townscape made up of nineteenth century wharves and warehouses which surround the early eighteenth century St Mary's Church. Over the last three years a number of the warehouses have been rehabilitated and converted to craft workshops, artist studios, flats and a picture reference library. The continuity of physical conservation has therefore been accompanied by an influx of new activities and a revitalisation of the area.

The residents of the Rotherhithe area have witnessed many changes over the last ten years especially from the closure of the Surrey Docks in 1970 and the closure of riverside wharves and warehouses. It is a tight-knit and stable local community but up to now few of the changes in the Conservation Area have been of particular benefit to the local community. An attractive river-side area that is open to the public could both enhance the Conservation Area and provide an amenity for the local residents.

Immediate Surroundings

Underneath 121–123 Rotherhithe Street lies the Thames Tunnel built by Marc Brunel (assisted by his son Isambard) between 1825 and 1843 and now used by the East London Line. The Brunel Exhibition Project is converting the Pump House across the road from 121–125 Rotherhithe Street into a museum to commemorate this great technological achievement and has landscaped the area in front of the Pump House. Other buildings inland of the site are Grice's Granary converted to a picture reference library and craft workshops and Swan Road Dwellings, one of the earliest examples of LCC housing (W.E. Riley 1907) and accommodating 129 households on only 1.3 acres. It is intended that the riverside walk along the South Bank of the Thames should through the conservation area follow the line of Rotherhithe Street and it is anticipated that at some time the section of Rotherhithe Street in front of this site will be pedestrianised. The boundary of the Conservation Area lies between 123 and 125 Rotherhithe Street.

Site Characteristics

125 Rotherhithe Street is 560 sqm with 28 m of river frontage and is owned by the GLC. At present it consists of an open yard flanked by buildings and sheds.

Development Objectives

1. To provide a useable riverside area with free public access that will prove attractive and interesting to both residents and visitors.
2. To take full advantage of river views.
3. To relate the development to its surroundings and to integrate it with the proposed riverside walk.

Constraints

1. The flood defence wall must be retained to its present height and at least its present strength.
2. There must be no loading near to the river wall.
3. Designs should initially be for 125 Rotherhithe Street alone but allow for a connection with the Brunel Exhibition Project's landscaping when Rotherhithe Street is predestrianised.
4. Climatic conditions by the river frequently include brisk cold winds.
5. Only hardy plants will grow in an exposed riverside position.
6. Maintenance requirements should be minimised.

Design ideas

There are numerous local themes which might prove attractive to designers. The historical associations of Rotherhithe with Gulliver, the Mayflower and the Brunels and with ship building, ship breaking and docking are some of the most obvious.

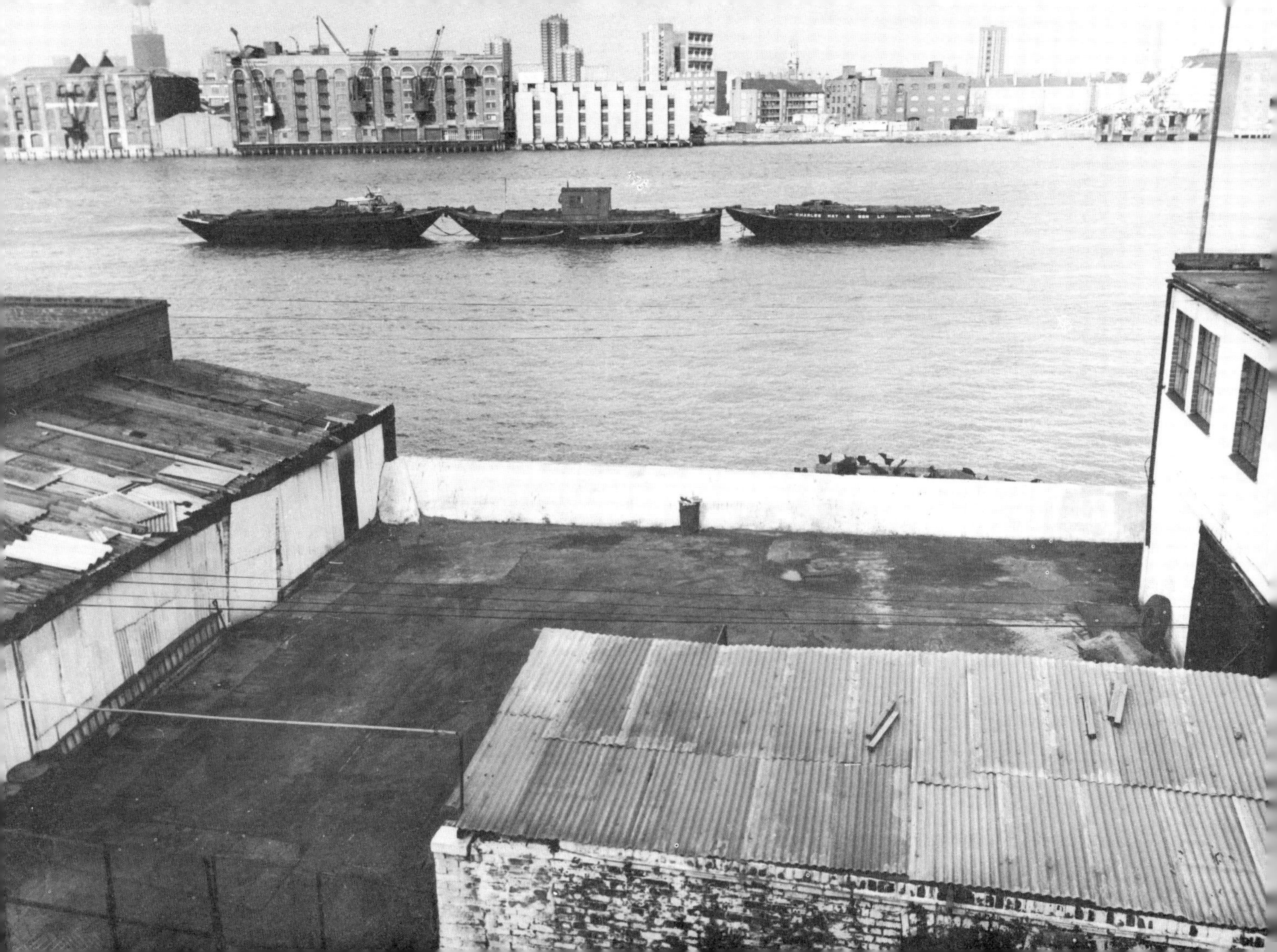

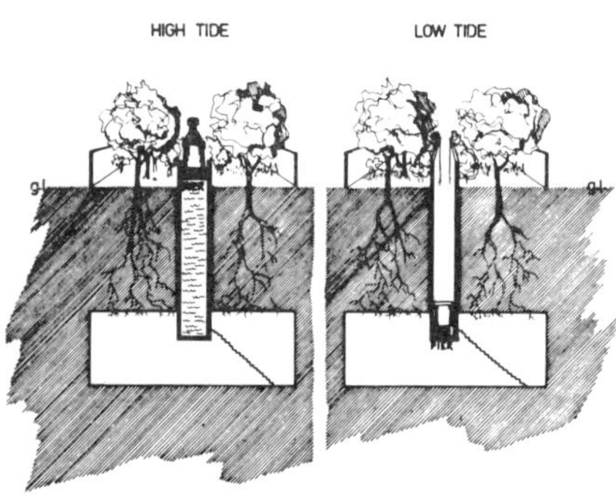

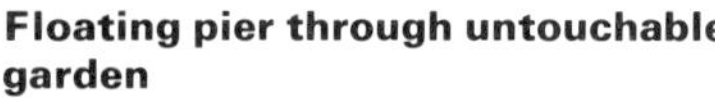

Floating pier through untouchable garden
John Andrews

A pier floats through a garden enclosed by a holed wall; the garden cannot be touched by hand or foot. Instead the pier, according to the level of the river, passes above and below the surface taking passengers to view parts set by the time of day. At low water the pier descends to the undergrowth where the garden's base rests, and passengers are taken to a dark hall the size of the garden above. Natural light is channelled down through narrow shafts, casting reflections on a ceiling of roots. A warning bell rings; it is time to return to the pier and be taken to the surface. The pier rises to the incoming river and a slow walk towards the pier head gives the sensation of leaving the ground and becoming riverborne. Passengers pass through an avenue of wind organs disguised as columns; the faster the wind—the stronger the sound; the higher the octave—the closer the pier head.

Born 1950 in London. Studied at Hammersmith School of Art and the Architectural Association.

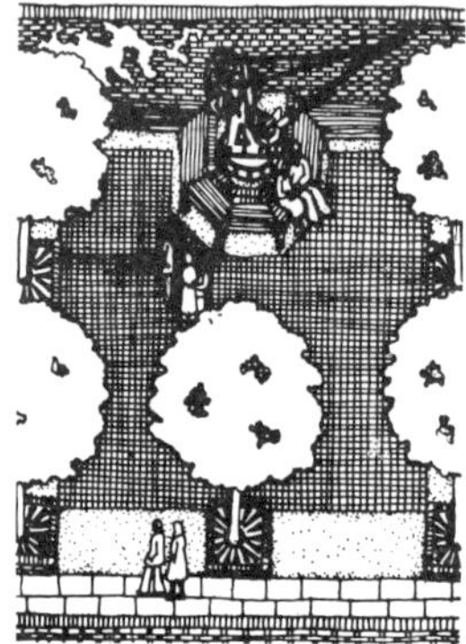

Brunel wharf
Peter Bartle

In the past the Thames has been cut off from Londoners by the industry and commerce that provided their employment. The movement of the docks downstream has reversed this situation and has led to proposals for 'opening up' the Thames, which could destroy the secret dockland character. My proposal tries to preserve this character whilst making the river more accessible. The site's scale precludes major recreational activity; it should function as a seating area for tourists and local residents. An essential feature of the design is the wall running along Rotherhithe Street, which allows limited views through the wharf. It is proposed to convert the existing 2-storey building into four shops serving local needs and providing unofficial policeing of the area. A piece of dock machinery will provide a focal point. The limited budget has led to the maximum use of existing features.

Born 1943 in Croydon. Studied architecture at the South Bank Polytechnic. Works as architect and freelance illustrator.

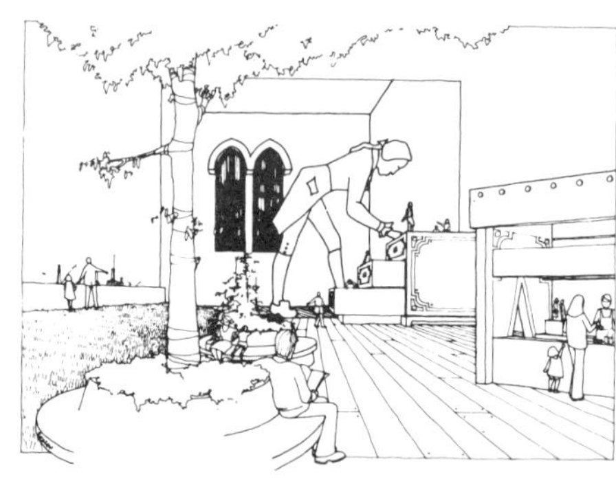

Gulliver's world
Meir Berk, Seving Berk

The problem: to provide a riverside area with public access attractive to residents and visitors and affording clear river views. The solution: to create an environment in which abrupt changes in scale transport the visitor to the two different worlds of dwarfs and giants which Gulliver experienced. The visitor becomes the dwarf in Gulliver's living room. Viewing platforms at different levels take the form of a chest of drawers while a soft drinks and ice cream bar hides under a stool. Gulliver's flower pots are planting boxes with seats around them and contain two mature trees. Inside the chest of drawers the visitor is the giant in an environment where special models and light effects recreate the adventures of Gulliver the dwarf.

Meir Berk born 1945 in Tel-Aviv. Studied at the State Academy of Fine Arts Department of Architecture, Istanbul and Thames Polytechnic. Seving Berk born 1945 in Turkey. Studied at the State Academy of Fine Arts Department of Architecture, Istanbul. Both work as architectural designers.

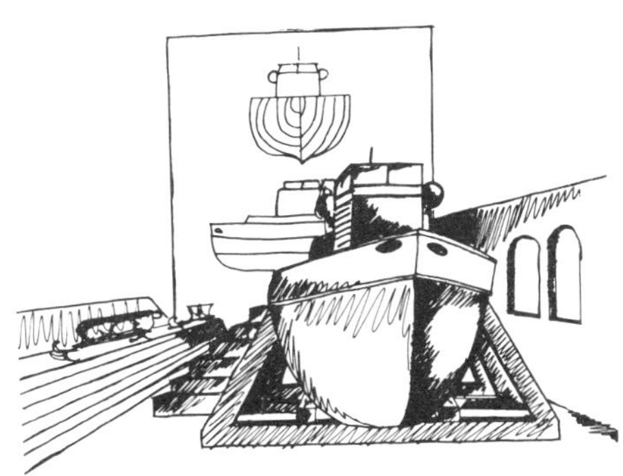

A tug for Southwark
Iain Boyd Whyte

The proposal is to install an old Thames tug on a wooden cradle, running along the centre of the site, parallel to the river. The tug would: 1. provide a reminder of a form of river traffic which is almost extinct; 2. be an indestructible plaything for children; the cradle would act as a climbing frame, and old ropes, hatch covers and other riverside bric-à-brac could be left around to add to the fun; 3. act as an elevated viewing platform, giving wide views of the river.
The tug motif would be reinforced by simple paintings of tugs and dockland scenes on the enclosing end walls. The painting should be crude and forceful, almost at the level of informed graffiti. A minimum of landscaping completes the scheme, which would be both an exciting playground and an informal monument to the commercial life of the Thames.

Born 1947 in Bexley, Kent. Studied at Nottingham, Cornell, Cambridge and Berlin Universities. Works as language teacher and is studying for a Ph.D.

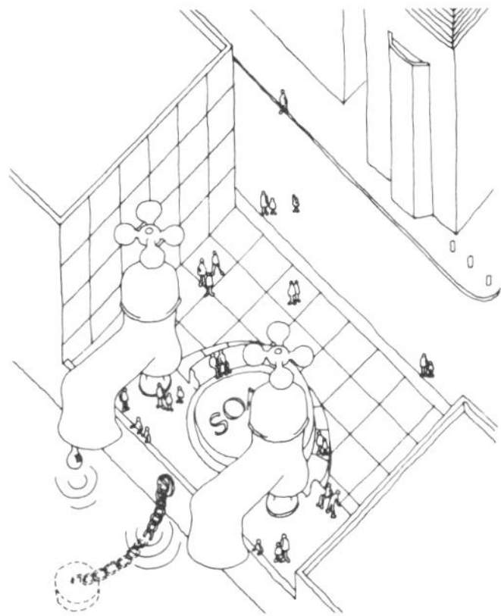

Thames basin
Ray Bryant, Peter Mason

A permanent structure of two 8 m high taps overhanging the river wall between two warehouses whose end walls are painted. An event where once a day water automatically discharges from the taps during the incoming of the tide until the basin is full. The water in the basin is retained by means of a plug and chain attached to the river wall. The public join in by using the water filled soap between the taps or just sitting on a toothbrush, sliding down a razor or jumping on an inflatable tube of toothpaste that are to be found on the checkered paving behind. The year of the Jubilee is celebrated and forever remembered, as the taps will of course be silver.

Ray Bryant born 1945 in Birmingham. Peter Mason born 1943 in Stoke-on-Trent. Both studied Leicester College of Art & Design. Both work as architects.

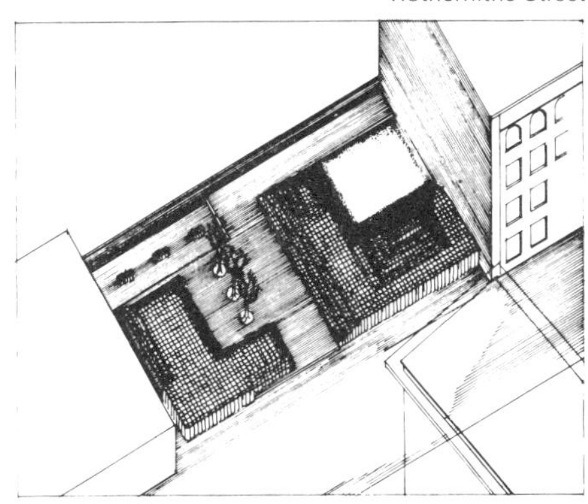

Dockland playground
Manlin Chee

The design is for adults and children—a relaxing, pleasing space for local residents and a contribution to the riverside walk. The timber baulks offer a reference to dockland and shipbuilding while being an impressive yet economical source of material. It is hoped that all material used will be secondhand, and paving and step levels made of London stock so as to relate to the surrounding buildings. Similar bricks to those of the Brunel pump house might be used, if available, to integrate this building in the design. If the required quantity of timber baulks, as found in wharves, is not available, railway sleepers might be used: their rectangular section could be put to advantage in forming patterns with the square sectional timber baulks. Timber would be sanded and impregnated in non-toxic wood preservative and all edges and sides champered or rounded a minimum of $\frac{1}{4}$".

Born 1951 in Singapore. Studies interior design at Chelsea School of Art.

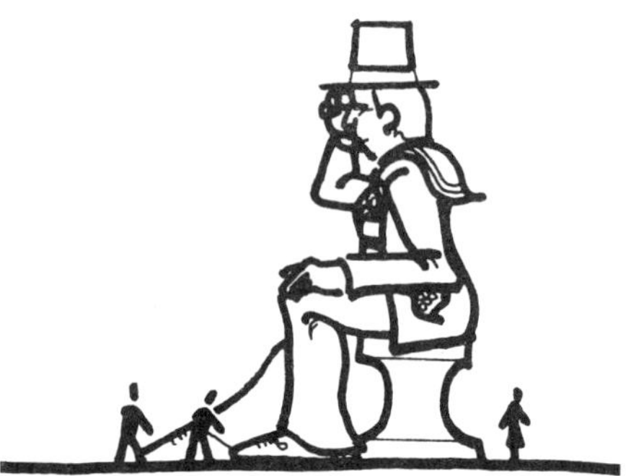

Sailor's viewpoint
W A Jacques

The associations of the site with Gulliver and the Mayflower inspired me to propose this scheme of a giant sailor seated in a hard landscaped area overlooking the river. The figure, dressed in the earliest style of Royal Naval uniform, would be in fact a prospect tower with a viewing platform in the head some 40ft above the ground giving a splendid panoramic view of the river and docklands all around.

Born 1942. Studied industrial design at Hornsey College of Art and architecture at Hammersmith. Works as architectural assistant.

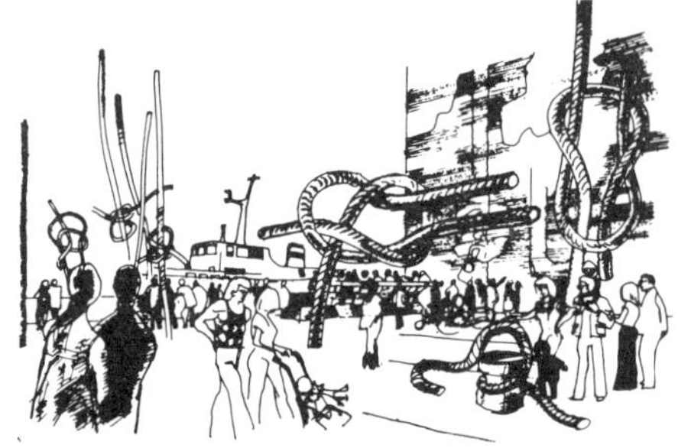

A Brobdingnagian knot garden
Thomas Meddings

A riverside theme of rope, knots and splicing magnified to recall Gulliver's voyage from Rotherhithe to the land of giants, furnishes a space for viewing, sitting, children's play and learning knots. Large knot models in core-reinforced rope impregnated with resin for rigidity and protection offer useful illustration supported by explanatory panels. The first priority is to make the riverside comfortably accessible. Planting is deliberately excluded and easily mantained surfaces are chosen, with brick paving to be extended across a pedestrianised Rotherhithe Street to the Brunel site. Rings, bollards and hooks can be salvaged from dockland and a replica of Brunel's Great Eastern cable would recall another example of giant scale with local connections. From Brandram Wharf's wall emerges a low-key mural of giant hands and ropes—carried out by local school children using standard colours on a brick-by-brick system.

Born 1922 in London. Studied architecture at the Regent Street Polytechnic. Works as architect.

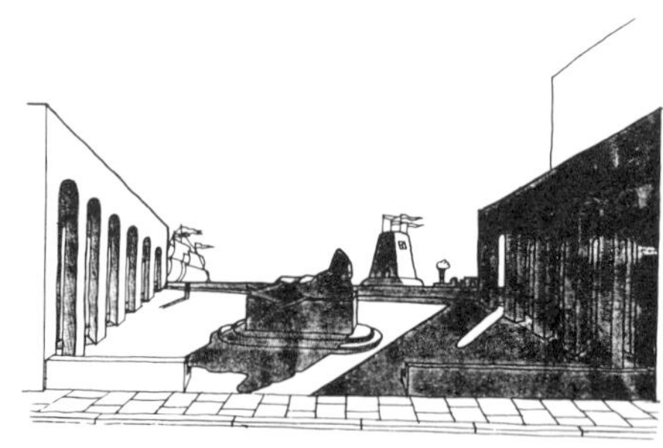

Souvenir d'Italie
Henry Medwell

The proposal is for an arcaded vista incorporating a children's playground. The idea is to use such visual devices as false perspective, changes in scale, artificial shadows, etc., to translate into 3-dimensional form the imagery of Giorgio de Chirico. Thus the scheme could be termed a 'folly' in the 18th century sense, where landscape architects attempted to construct scenic prospects inspired by the paintings of artists such as Claude and Poussin.

Born 1942 in Surrey. Works as hotel caretaker.

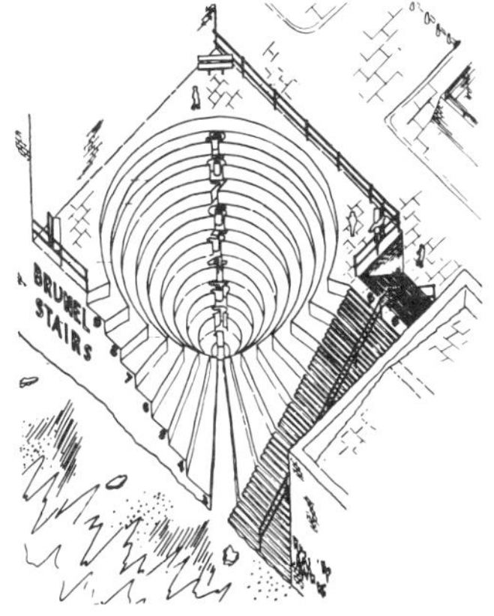

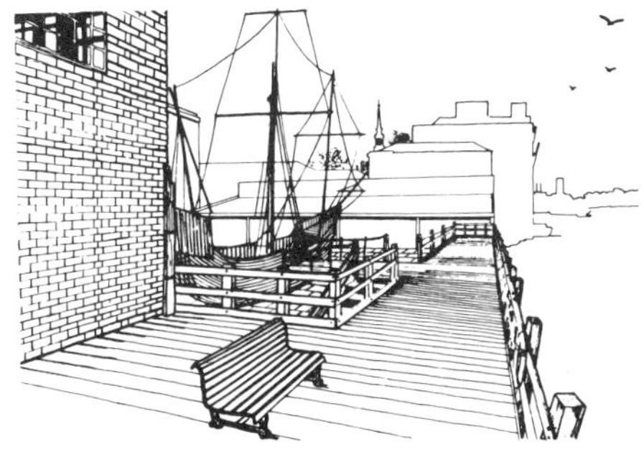

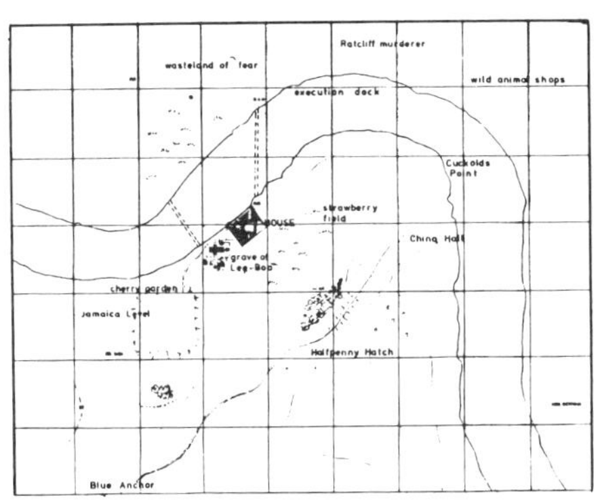

Brunel stairs and tide indicator
Roger Morgan

Any community in close contact with the sea needs and acquires a close understanding of, and harmony with, its ebb and flow, but owing to the increasing decay of riverside warehouses, docks and quays, public access to and contact with the Thames as a living and useful entity has ceased. My proposal enables small boats to be freely launched and recovered by the public, and beachcombers to have free access to the foreshore. Incorporated is a state-of-the-tide indicator, which doubles as a landing and mooring stage when the tide is partly in. A public promenade round the top has an open view of the Thames due to the cut down in the river wall and will incorporate tidal predictions for the year, and an explanation of the tides. Finally it provides a link between the Brunel Exhibition project and the river, echoing the medieval water-gates which once linked all important riverside sites with the water.

Born 1948 in Shirley, Warwicks. Studied architecture at Manchester University. Works as architect and inventor.

All at sea
James Muir, Michael Turney

Two considerations guide our proposals: i. The young mothers in the Swan Road Dwellings badly need somewhere for their children to play.; ii. there is a need for relatively low-rent business premises in the area. Proposal 1. The substantial two-storey building on the site should be refurbished and let to a small commercial enterprise such as a jobbing printer, sign writer, etc. This building would be suited to a small crafts industry like a pottery, weaving shed or glass works, but only if the craftsmen were prepared to take in apprentices from the borough. 2. In the middle of the site we would erect a colourful, robustly-built ship for the kids to play on, and in, and over. 3. Over the flood wall a wooden walkway should be constructed giving fine views of the river. 4. Take down the gates!

James Muir born 1952 in London. Studied at University College. Works as researcher for television.

Michael Turney born 1945 in London. Studied at St Dunstan's College. Works in television scenic design.

Traces of an amusement arcade for the generation of fragments in time
Rodney Place, Patricia Pringle

Portions of the amusement arcade for the generation of sensible pleasure. When all materials will last for near eternity, customers give themselves up to the creation of a world where decay is permitted, even inevitable. The ruin-pleasure sought is the reassurance of footsteps worked in stone. Events mark the flow of time. Proof of consumption is proof of existence; it postulates the possibility of a past. This past's reality for us is surely unknown to the customers of the ruin-arcade who even now are slipping tokens into the slot machines, strolling wide-eyed past fictional landscapes—moments of history made for their pleasure, which slide like debris into our world. How their fantasies pollute our past! All this will presently be, but now water fills the halls and holds them still.

Rodney Place born 1952 in Johannesburg. Patricia Pringle born 1952 in Belfast. Both study at the Architectural Association.

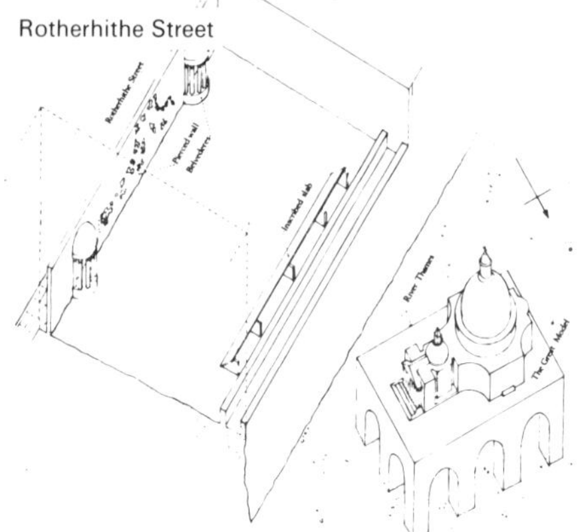

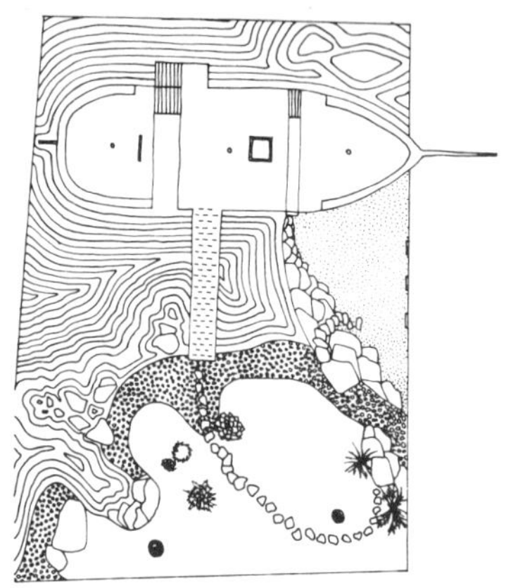

Pierced wall
Fred Scott

The proposal is for a pierced wall; a slab with an inscription to be placed within the site, near the river wall, parallel to and facing the wall; and an enlarged reproduction of the Great Model design for St Paul's to be placed on a platform in the Thames. The wall is pierced with the pattern of half the plan of the model. There are two belvederes attached to the river side of the wall, entered by steps through the wall from the street. It is made of smooth concrete. The site is cleared but not levelled and is then scorched to promote in particular the growth of willowherb. The abundant ecology of such sites is well known; no planting should be needed, and the only maintenance the occasional clearing of litter. The slab is marble and carries the inscription: "This great model was Christopher Wren's favourite design for St Paul's Cathedral. He was prevented from building it by the clergy. It stands as a warning to all artists."

Born in 1939. Studied at the Royal College of Art. Teaches at the Architectural Association.

Three windows on the Thames
E C Sinclair

The concept starts from a literal interpretation of the original title given to the Rotherhithe site 'Window on the Thames'. Three circular panes of reinforced glass set into the river wall allow the visitor to see underwater; they are actual windows onto the river. From this situation the visitor can see a ship's hull looming alongside. The ship is landlocked, but raked sand simulates a body of water and there is an island to which the ship is 'moored'. The style of the ship's layered decks is roughly based on a projected design of the 'Mayflower' and the island represents the inhospitable shore of the New World.

Born 1949 in Toronto, Canada. Studied at the University of Alberta and London University. Works as primary school teacher.

Wall at Art Education Building

'Up the wall and round the bend' – a mural to focus on an Arts Complex in central Sheffield

1. The competition is for the treatment of the flanking walls of the Hay's Building, overlooking the Crucible Theatre forecourt. Hay's Building is used as an art education centre for exhibitions, lectures etc. It forms part of an established civic and cultural sector of Sheffield city centre, which is proposed as a Conservation Area. The Crucible Theatre, The Lyceum Theatre, The Town Hall extensions, St. Maries Church, Victoria Hall, the Unitarian Church, Central Library and Graves Art Gallery are all situated close to the site.

2. The wall can be considered in three parts, as shown in the elevations.

Wall A is 17m length × 8m height
Wall B is 14m length × 6m height
Wall C is 13m length × 6m height

A gable end above wall A (8m length by 8m height) may also be included in the design or may be treated as a separate entity. In addition to the changes in direction between walls A, B and C there are many smaller variations in direction and height. Other features such as fire escape, telephone box, name plates and the ground surface at the foot of the walls should also be taken into account.

3. It is important that proposals for implementing the mural are included in the submission and that the competitor or his representative is available to direct work. It is hoped that arrangements can be made to implement the chosen entry during Summer 1977.

4. The design (or designs) may be two or three dimensional in concept – or a combination of both – depending upon which part of the wall surface is being considered.

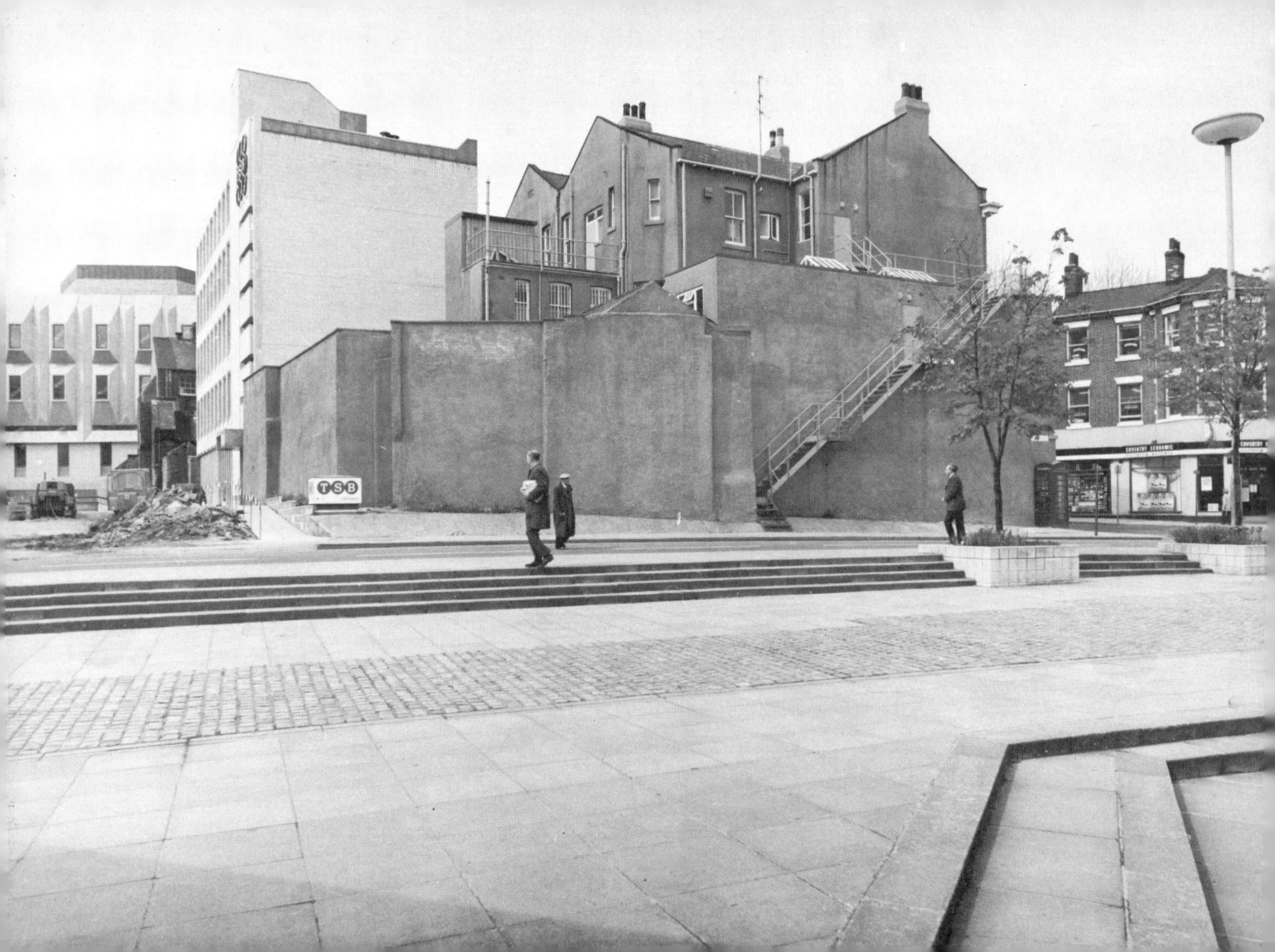
TSB
COVENTRY ECONOMIC

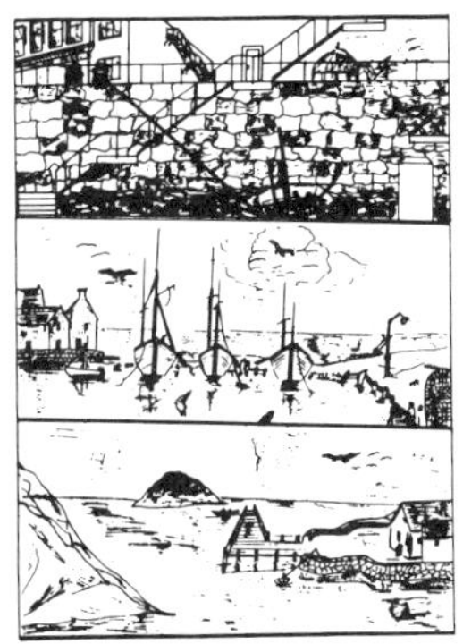

Sheffield seascape
Devonn Allison

When I first thought of the problem posed by the walls of the Sheffield building I realised I had to incorporate staircase, telephone-box, name-plate, etc. At present I am depicting a seascape; wall A is the harbour, wall B is the estuary and wall C is the view out to sea. I have tried to create a slow-moving, calm, peaceful picture ideal for sea-lovers. I purposely chose to design a seascape as a contrast to the fast, noisy city life which I imagine going on around my painting. The recesses and angles of the rooftops of the Sheffield building help to enhance my picture but pose very difficult problems. I have not yet exhausted all the possibilities, but hope that all my ideas will come together in my final entry.

Born 1961 in London. Attends Stockwell Manor School.

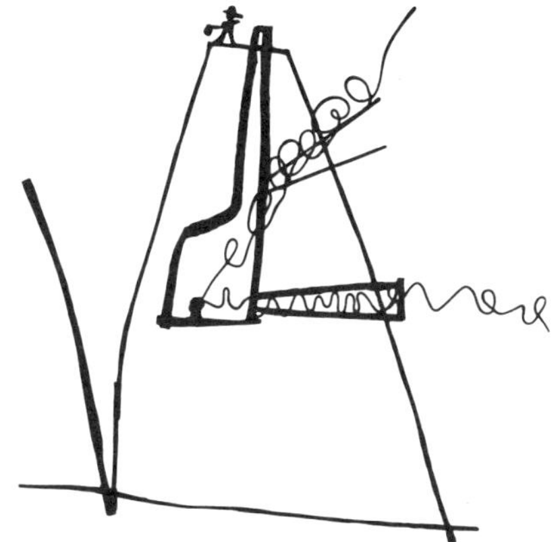

Blow Starsky and Hutch!
Raymond Arnatt

I thought that as this is an art education building it would be appropriate to use ideas from children, since this is where art education begins. I have used drawings made by my two children aged 9 and 6 years. I selected, and in some cases rearranged, all three walls (the gable end could contain the name of the building). Alternatives: 1. The metal sculptures to be fixed on a painted, white wall background (including the fire escape). 2. The metal sculptures to be fixed on coloured backgrounds, which are defined by the change in wall direction. The wall surface is extraordinary in the way that it changes direction and the best way to emphasise this is to treat it like a prism with intense colour kept to the narrow bands. Another consideration is one of durability. This proposal can be repainted at any time. The steel sculptures would be made in my studio and would be fixed with expanding bolts.

Born 1934 in Nuneham Courtenay, Oxon. Studied at the Oxford School of Art and the Royal College of Art. Works as a sculptor.

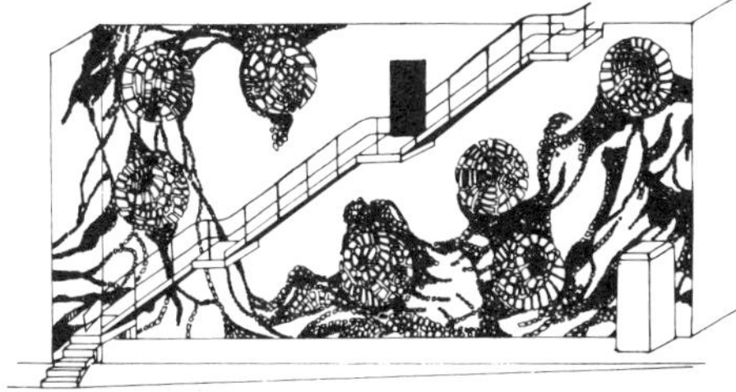

Without beginning, without end
Nigel Cartlidge

Constructed by inlaying broken used paving stones in pigmented concrete, rising at the most two inches from surface of wall, but varied heights to give a textural quality to help the image to move in varying lights. I see the wall as a link for landlocked Sheffield with the sea. Which has been, and will come again.

Born 1952 in Cardiff. Studies fashion textiles at Birmingham Polytechnic Constructed Textile School.

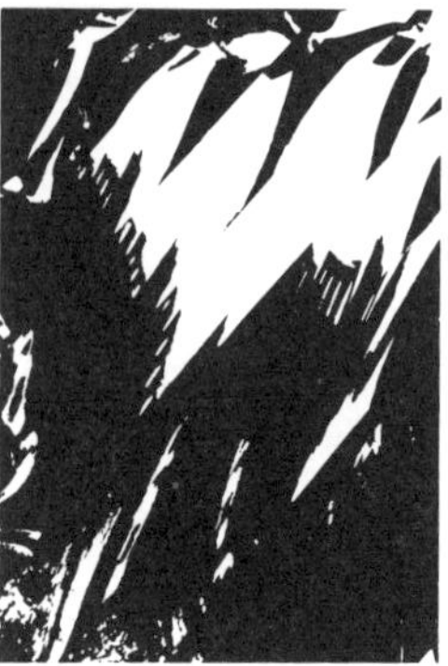

Sheffield steel wall
Mick Coleshaw

Art is to be found not only in the studios, but also in the industrial workshops throughout the country.

Sheffield is no exception, and the artistry and skill of its workmen is internationally acknowledged as many products of great beauty daily leave the city for the world's markets.

The arts complex reflects this integration between the community's culture and industry.

Therefore the proposal is to present the wall, not with a static mural, but with an everchanging image in which the viewer, his family, his community and the buildings of commerce, faith and the arts will be reflected and synthesized. This will be achieved by cladding the wall with highly reflective stainless steel strips twisted diagonally across the faces of the building.

Born 1948 in Nottingham. Studies furniture design at Trent Polytechnic.

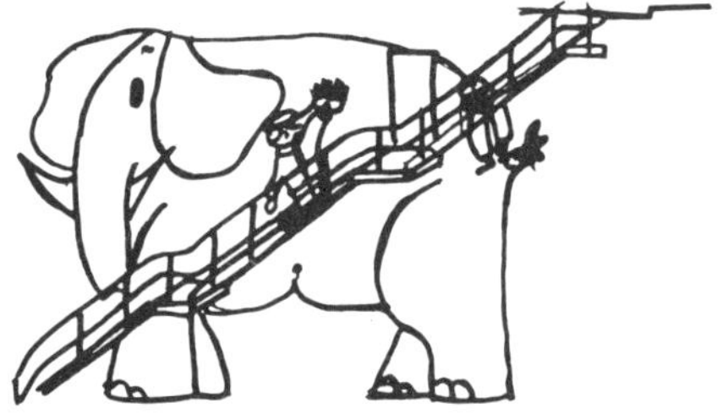

Rainbow zoo
Sarah Evans

I called my entry Rainbow zoo because the animals are to be painted all the bright colours of the rainbow. They are simple cartoon type animals. I thought that possibly the Art College students could have fun painting them on the walls of the building. Bright, washable, hard-wearing paint for outside would be used. I think the bright and colourful cartoon type animals I have drawn could be interesting and fun for the people passing by and using the college and other buildings around about. I drew the large pink elephant on the main wall because of the ladder which is just right for the keepers to stand on to clean him which is what they are doing. The lion reminds me of my cat fishing with one of his claws as a hook to catch the goldfish. All the other animals are also drawn to fit in with the shape of the building; the giraffe with his long neck going round the corner. The snake wriggling up the small thin panel on the wall.

Born 1965 in Lusaka, Zambia. Attends Walton High School, Stafford.

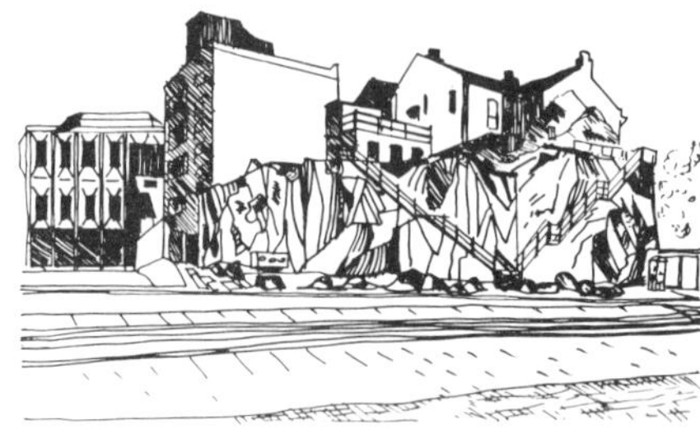

Sheffield cliffs
John Gingell

The site is unusual in a city—a house perched on top of a wall. The proposal seeks to extend this constructive fact into a visual reality of 'cliff face' by painting such a reference over the wall face. The ladder staircase will be echoed in the painting and to some extent the logic will be reinforced by stones laid into the base area at pavement level. Some perspective feeling will occur in the painting so that the approach to the site will be one of interplay with 2-dimensional illusion and 3-dimensional reality.

Born in Welling, Kent. Studied at Goldsmiths' College School of Art. Lectures in fine art at the South Glamorgan Institute of Higher Education Faculty of Art and Design.

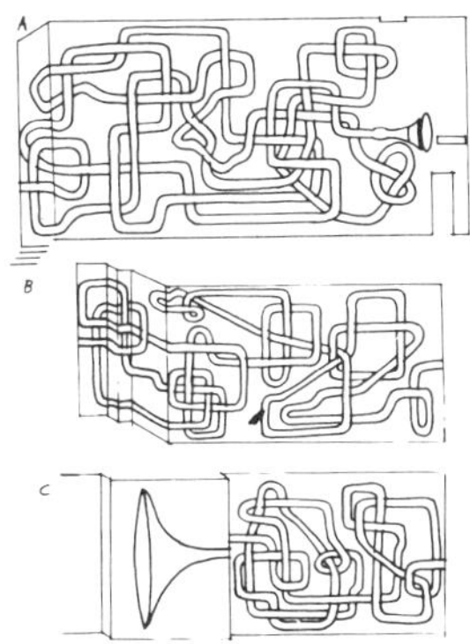

Wall of brass
David Jones

The design I have done is of a brass instrument. I got this idea from a poster of wall paintings in Cincinnati and from my friend at Holmewood who plays a French horn. I made a combination of the two ideas to fit the requirements of the Sheffield Wall.

Born 1964 in Speldhurst, Kent. Attends Holmewood House School, near Tunbridge Wells.

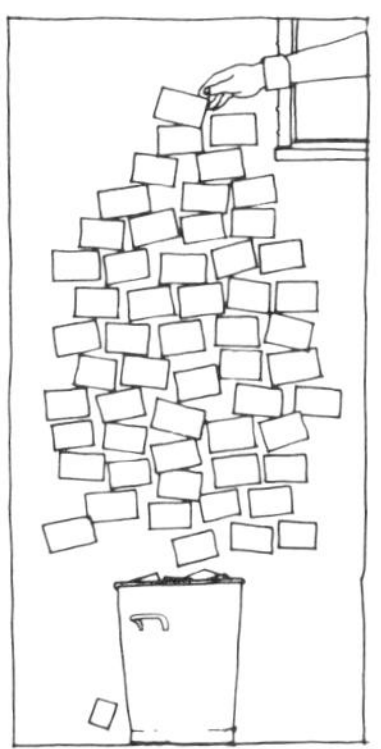

Funscape
Low, Mansarde and Hash Associates

A funscape is a joyous or mirthful idea superimposed on an ugly building. The block of listed buildings of which the Hay's Building (1876) is the most prominent is orientated back-to-front in the context of later adjoining buildings such as the Central Library (1932), the Crucible Theatre (1970) and the Town Hall extension (1977). Plans to extend Hay's Building in materials matching surrounding buildings had to be abandoned in 1974 for lack of finance. The present competition offers a second chance to tidy up an important city centre area. The selected design would be implemented by recruits from a local college of art under the supervision of the Associates.

The five toilers in the architectural field (3 architects and 2 architectural technicians, born between 1939 and 1952), who comprise the informal, pseudonymous association, have been aware, since their separate furrows first coincided at Sheffield, that an ever-deepening rut would engulf them unless they changed direction.

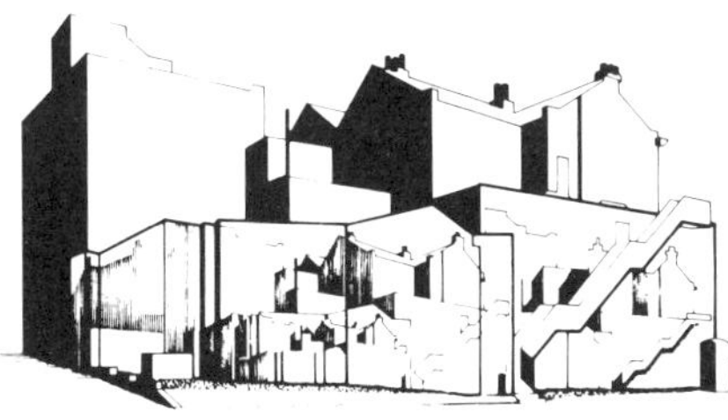

Self-reflecting perspectives
Alan McKim Boyce, Keith Garbett

The proposed design is intended to reduce and comment on the mass of the buildings above and beyond the retaining walls by turning the walls themselves into an introspective 'foredrop', which in turn reflects the theatrical association of the area. The final design would be detailed on site by those executing the work under the guidance of the designers. Each facet of the podium to be treated from its own viewpoint and, whilst the whole facade would initially form a single coherent design, it is hoped that individual panels would be repainted at intervals to introduce other, locally designed, elements.

Alan McKim Boyce born 1938. Studied at the Central School. Works as industrial designer and lecturer.

Keith Garbett born 1936. Studied at the School of Architecture, Cambridge. Works as architect.

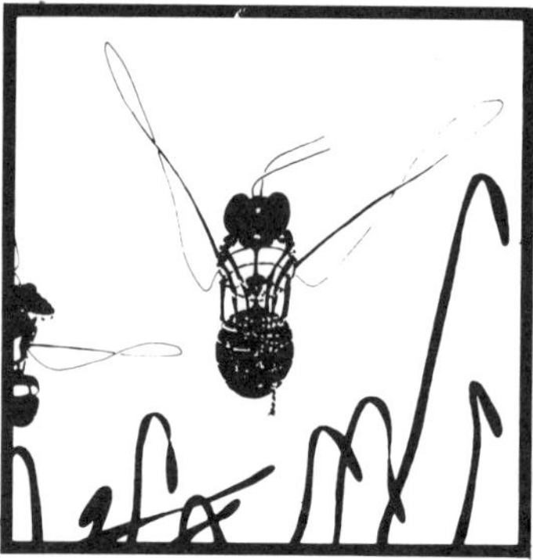

Grass
Alan Millar

The black disc is supposed to be the sun which is cut away, as in 'cut-away drawing', as it turns the corner . . . that's all. . . .

Born 1954 in Falkirk. Post graduate studies at the Glasgow School of Art Mackintosh School of Architecture.

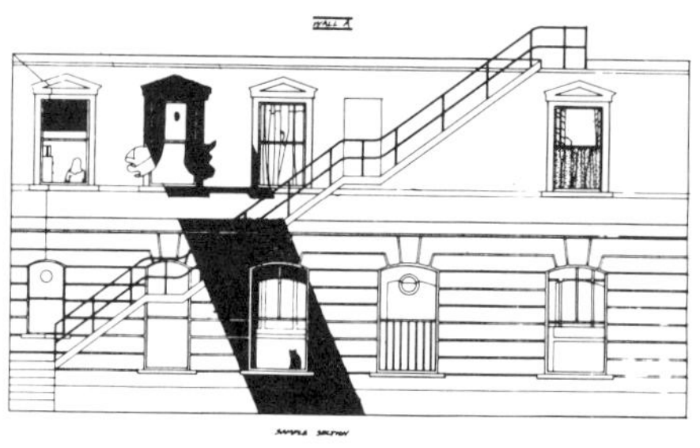

Windows
Paul Morris

Every window tells a story.

Born 1945. Studied graphic design, film and television at the Royal College of Art. Works as designer and lectures at Gwent College of Further Education.

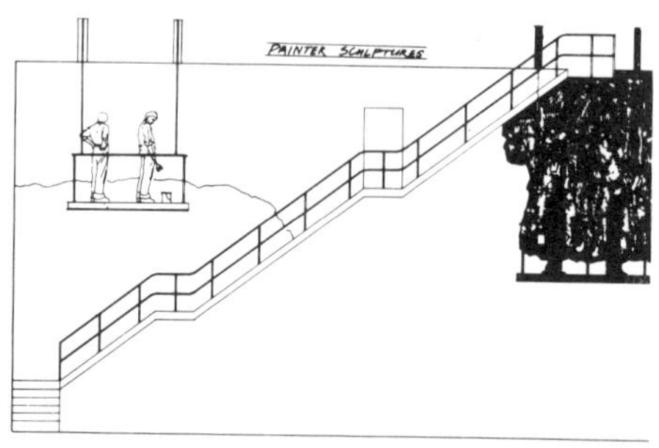

Painter sculpture
Paul Morris

The sculptures are life-sized workmen suspended on cradles fixed to the wall. They are painting the wall in preparation for an artist to paint a mural. But they are each using a different colour.
For biographical note see 121

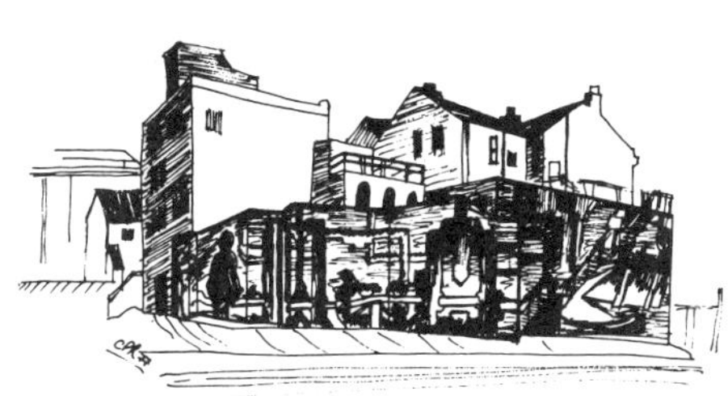

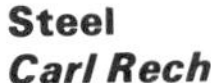

Steel
Carl Rech

The mural attempts to symbolise the interior workings of a steel mill. Despite recent upheavals, the steel industry is inextricably tied to the origins of Sheffield as a community, and in many ways is a vital source of pride. It constitutes the city's lifeblood— indirectly the lifeblood of the cultural amenities (such as the Crucible Theatre) which surround the wall. The bright reds and oranges of heat and light, contrasted with the dark machinery, would provide a stimulating picture in keeping with the bright lights and paintwork of the Crucible Theatre. The fire escape would be incorporated into the colour scheme to represent a staircase within the steelworks.

Born 1955 in Bury, Lancashire. Studied geography at Sheffield University. Now studies landscape design at Newcastle University.

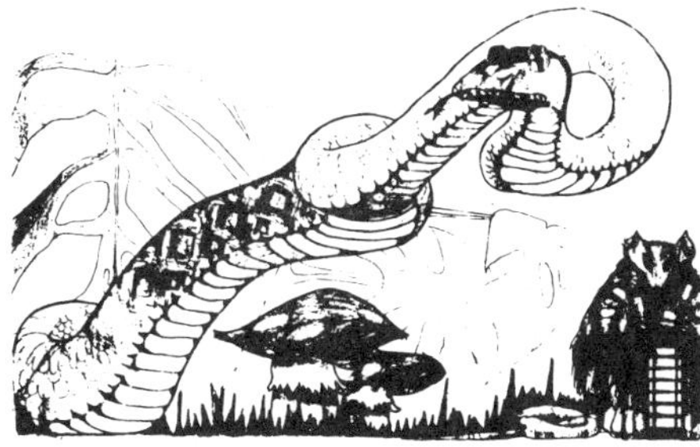

Boa constructor
Keith Robinson

The mural uses natural elements as a total contrast to man-made eyesores. All the images, from the blazing desert to the steaming jungle, represent the hostility of the natural world towards the built environment and challenge man's complacent occupation of the city. The snake, the rat, even toadstools are redolent of danger, disease, pain and death—their presence in an urban situation is an act of defiance. The snake conceals the eyesore of the fire escape behind a sinuous outline, emphasised by its position a few feet in front of the wall. The rat, unable to devour the telephone kiosk, shows its displeasure quite clearly.

Born 1946 in Bredbury. Studied architecture at Nottingham University. Works as architect.

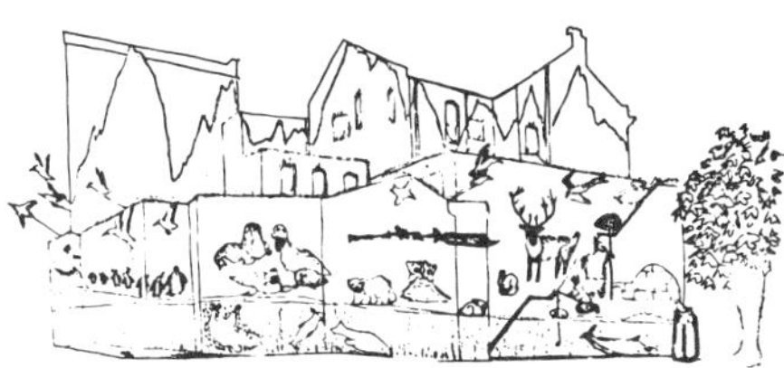

Frosty Friday in Sheffield Wednesday
Soraya Smithson

If it is ever painted, I hope that the people living in the houses behind my Sheffield wall, Arctic scene, will consent to let the backs of their houses be painted white and silvery-grey like I have shown in my drawing. I have tried to make it as lively as possible and to make it fit slightly in with its surroundings. I have drawn a bird in a nest on top of the telephone box, and birds flying away from the picture on springy wires that will move in the wind. The animals that I have drawn in my picture, the White Owl, the Polar Bears, the Penguin, the Whale, the White Rabbits, the Reindeers, the Harp Seals, the Seagull and of course the Eskimoes and the Husky Team and Igloo, all come from the Arctic. The Arctic in the summer is normally crowded as I have shown because the winter is six months of continuous night and nearly all the animals are asleep so you do not see them.

Born 1964 in London. Attends Pimlico Comprehensive.

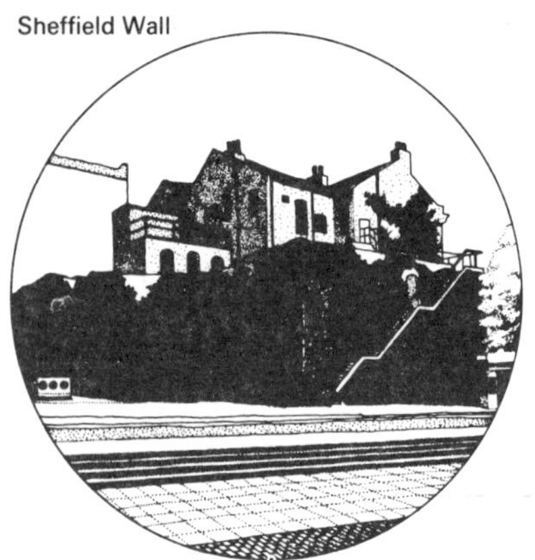

Stuff the genius loci?
Derek Walker Associates

A mural, in the normal sense of the word, is not always the solution to the problem of making ugly blank walls visually acceptable. Why not completely clothe the walls in ivy and paint bright red the fire escape stair and door, metal balustrades and telephone box? If feasible in terms of ownership and cost, the group of buildings above the wall could also be painted— or covered in ivy. The proposal came from a desire to produce a simple solution in concept, execution and maintenance; to produce a changing, growing solution, responsive to the seasons but equally acceptable at all times of year and in all weathers, to soften with planting the hard lines of the wall and introduce more plant material in the square; to put forward a design solution which will not become tedious, with overexposure, to the people using the surrounding facilities. Suggested planting methods are aimed at establishing fast, even coverage, while ensuring an interim appearance which is attractive while becoming mature.
Architectural practice.

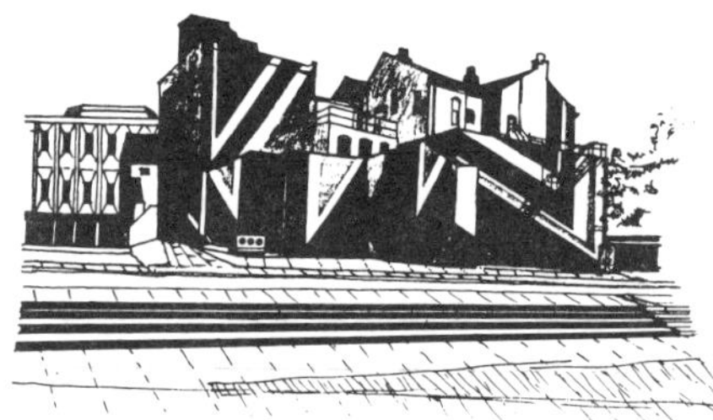

Royal chevron
Ron M Walker

The design is derived from a fragmented Union Jack— the aim being to commemorate Jubilee Year and to produce a strong, simple design using angular shapes to preserve and enhance the good proportions and expanse of wall available. The design would be interesting and make sense when viewed from any angle. This design could be easily executed on site. Red, white and blue would be the basic colour scheme, but this would vary between areas of flat colour and pointilist overlays. I have included the tall building in the rear as this seems a natural follow-through and gives a greater sense of completion or 'climax' to the whole work. The changes in direction of the walls will contribute naturally through the changing light of the day, to changes in the colours of the design.

Born 1935 in Calcutta. Studied at Stafford and Birmingham Colleges of Art. Works as artist and teaches art at Alleynes High School, Uttoxeter.

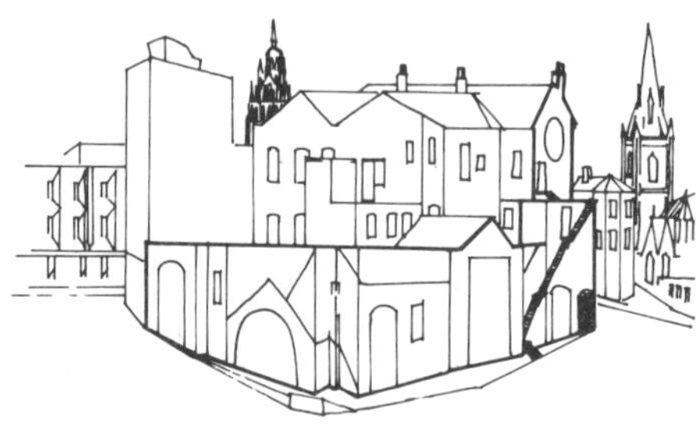

Sheffield sharrawaggi
Tony Whelan

The wall: It's a collection of happy accidents (which is what *sharrawaggi* means) and must never lose its human scale and architectural roots. I want to provide a basic framework of familiar shapes and grade the colours from a whisper at the ends to a shout in the middle— and I want other people to use the 'doors' for posters, graffiti and mini-murals of a topical nature.

Born 1937 in Liverpool. Training: night classes at St Helens School of Art after an abortive diploma first year. Works as scenic designer and technical lecturer at the Royal Scottish Academy of Music and Drama, having been a publishers' galley clerk, sailing instructor, rescue coxswain, model maker, stagehand, property maker, photographer, unemployed and production assistant at the Royal Opera House.

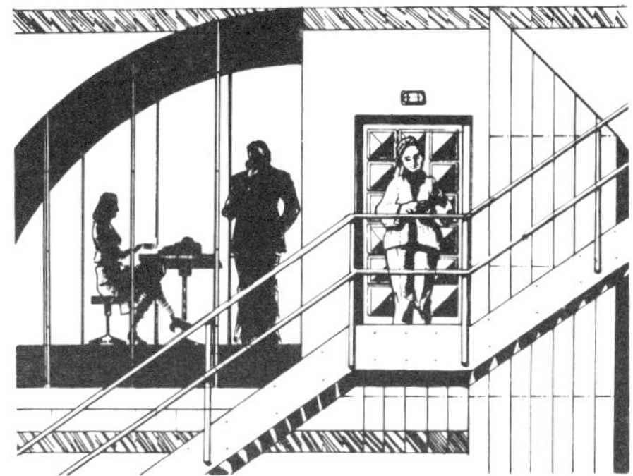

Scenes from city life
Graeme Willson, James Musgrave

Each panel is self-contained but at the same time there exists a continuum, with certain characters recurring. Thus, the whole work may be read from left to right as follows: 1. The Incident: a fight is taking place between two citizens, the new Sheffield Town Hall Extensions and the surrounding hills can be seen through the architecture. 2. The Riot: a clash between police and demonstrators. 3. & 4. Reconciliation and Burial: a small group of people gather to witness the burial of a friend. The left hand scene is partially viewed again from the side, through a door. 5. The Precinct: Two harlequin figures draw aside the curtains on the stage of life. We have attempted to depict as objectively as possible a slice-of-life. The subject of our work is the relationship of individuals to environment (as well as to each other) i.e figure to architectural space.

Graeme Willson born 1951 in N Yorkshire. Studied at Reading University. Is a full-time painter.

James Musgrave born 1956 in Scunthorpe. Studies graphics at Leeds Polytechnic.

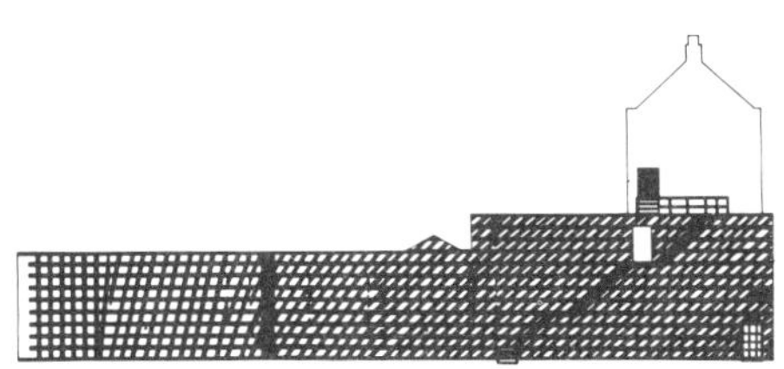

Red and green
Robyn Zayadi

Green and red are used in a tightly knit design. The geometric approach was dictated by the need to unify the three main surfaces by applying a sequential grid where the horizontal is retained and the vertical varies according to each section. The size of the vertical horizontal grid was determined by the width of the narrowest wall strip. The gradient grid on the wall beneath the gable was determined by the slope of the fire escape. All intermediate sections conform to a progressive gradient system as an integral part of the design.

Born 1946 in Sydney, Australia. Studied at the National Art School, Sydney. Teaches art.

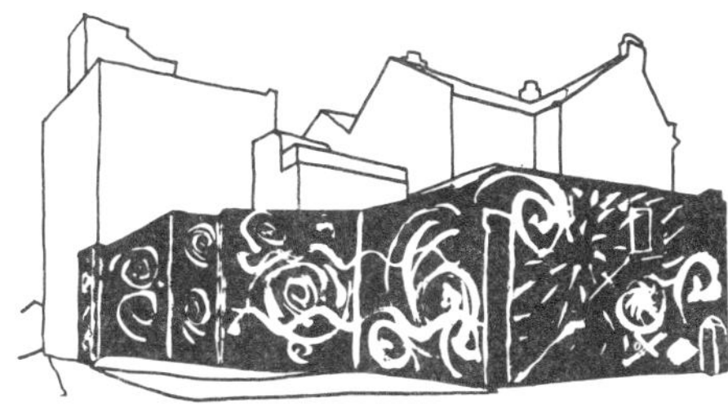

Whoosh!
Ingrid Zunde

A mural with a suitably lively theme to go next to an equally exciting theatre. Black was chosen to seem appropriate both at night and during the day as a background to a firework display of colour.

Born 1965 in Walsall. Attends Sheffield High School for Girls.

Playscape for Eastbourne, Stockton-on-Tees

Open space off Durham Road, Stockton

1. The Durham Road site is triangular in shape, being bounded by the Stockton/Newcastle Railway line, Lustrum Beck, and rear of properties fronting on to Durham Road itself. It has an area of some 4.9 hectares, 12 acres, although the final line of the south west boundary has yet to be precisely delineated.

2. The land is presently in the ownership of British Rail, but in 1975 the Borough of Stockton-on-Tees entered into a lease agreement for the land. The lease is for a guaranteed period of 3 years, with a termination period of three months notice from either side after that time. The Chief Planning Officer is currently preparing terms for the extension of the lease arrangement on a long term basis.

3. In 1975 the Council embarked on a scheme of improvement of the Durham Road land. This reclamation work is almost complete. The land is now a large gently sloping grassed area but with practically no landscaping and no formal facilities for play, passive recreation, or for sport. In addition, access to the land is very limited, as can be seen from the attached plan, with vehicular access only possible from the south west.

4. The land area does, however, represent a much needed recreational resource for an older inner urban housing area lacking in adequate play and recreational facilities. The housing areas to the north have suffered from adolescent vandalism and it is the Council's earnest hope that by providing "adventuresome" play facilities on this cleared land the incidence of vandalism may be reduced by the provision of healthier outlets for youthful energy.

5. Competitors are invited to put forward their general proposals for the treatment of the site area *as a whole* but to reserve their special attention for the detailed treatment of the northern end of the site as a base for a challenging play area.

6. As the contour plans indicate, the site area has a pronounced slope and it is felt appropriate to respond to this by adding further landscaping to produce a dominant and commanding feature in the landscape.

7. Within the general idea of a play area ideas are being sought for a form of playground that suits the particular locality, responds to the interesting site levels and is of a robust character.

8. It is not the intention of the Stockton-on-Tees Borough Council to provide buildings or formal play leadership arrangements, the play area should be so designed as to "fend for itself" and not require extensive and regular maintenance.

9. Whilst it is appreciated that children of all ages will be attracted by the play area, special attention should be paid to the requirements and interests of children above the age of nine or ten years of age.

10. The Council would expect to provide items of normal play equipment but competitors are encouraged to think of ways in which discarded or redundant building materials may be used. (Stockton has a long Railway heritage and the Council has for example made imaginative use in the past of old railway sleepers in stockade formation and retrieved old brick setts and granite paviors from old back streets).

11. Essentially the Council do not want "just another play area", the site is a challenging and interesting one and the object of the competition is to find an entry that provides *a very distinctive "place", a tough and resilient base for active play and a positive contribution to the enhancement of an area that has for too long been an ignored and ugly part of the town.*

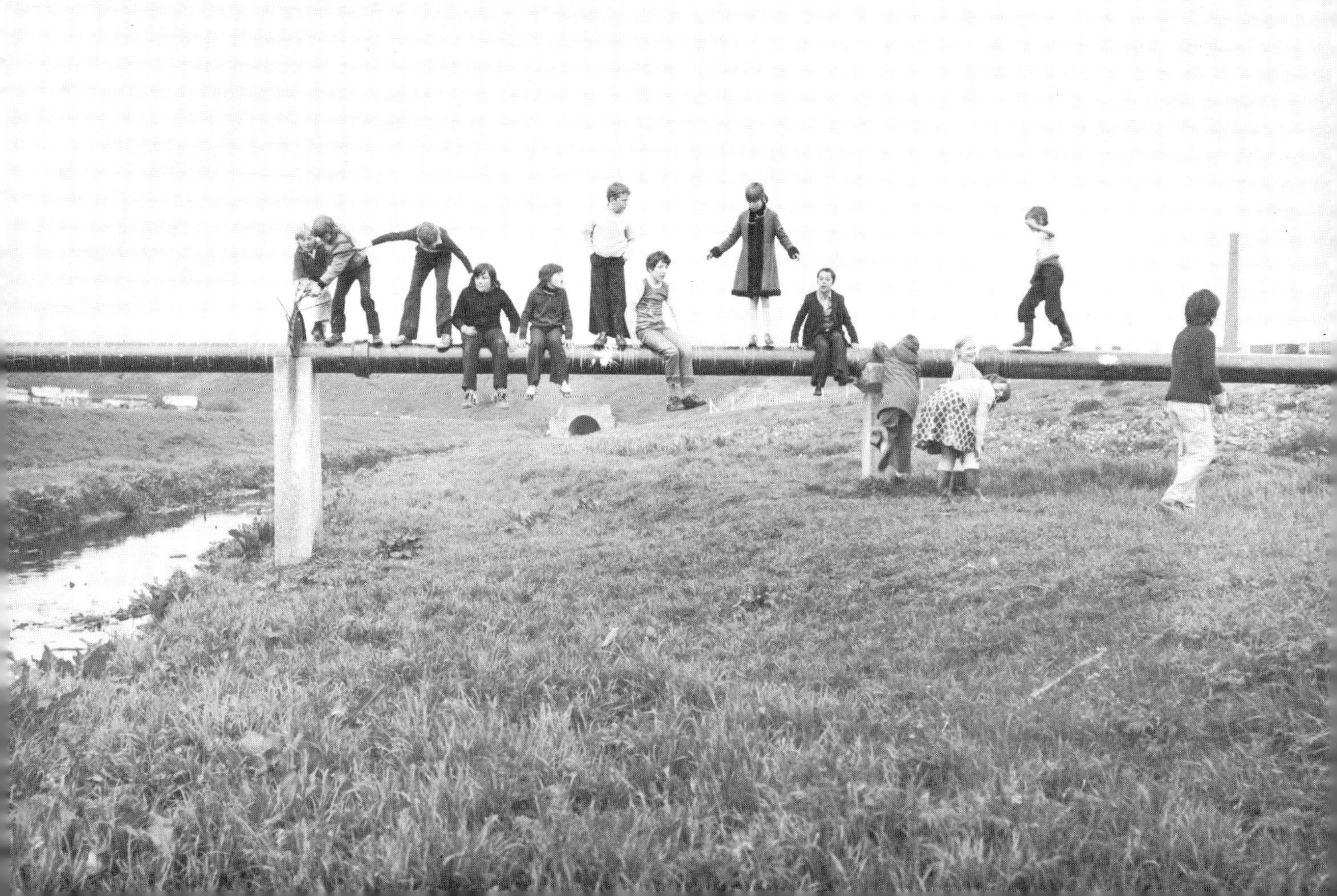

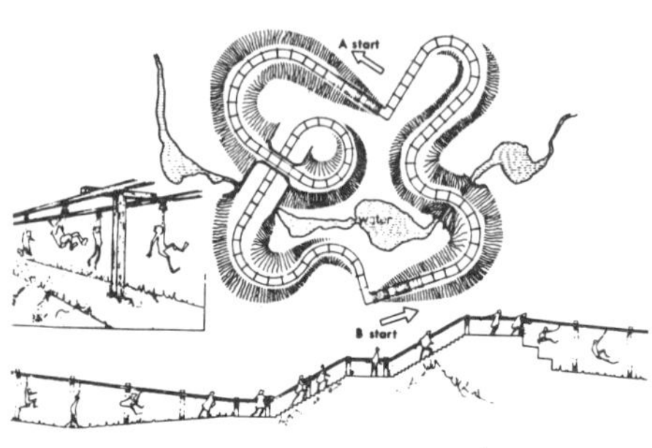

Monorail handslide
Julian Brafman

The two extra long slides of my proposed handslide system are intended to stretch a child physically. The anthropometric design will allow a child of any size to drop off the slide at any point quite safely. Any handpiece abandoned in the middle of a slide would free-fall, through gravity, to the end of the slide. At that point the track raises up the steps and the monorail starts again; thus a continuous loop is formed. The monorail is fitted with a variety of handpieces to cater for children of different sizes and includes a safety loop to carry physically handicapped children. The system is designed to make use of disused railway parts and thus the monorails consist of inverted railway tracks fitted to a 'T' section made from wooden track-sleepers.

Born 1953 in London. Studies interior design at Middlesex Polytechnic.

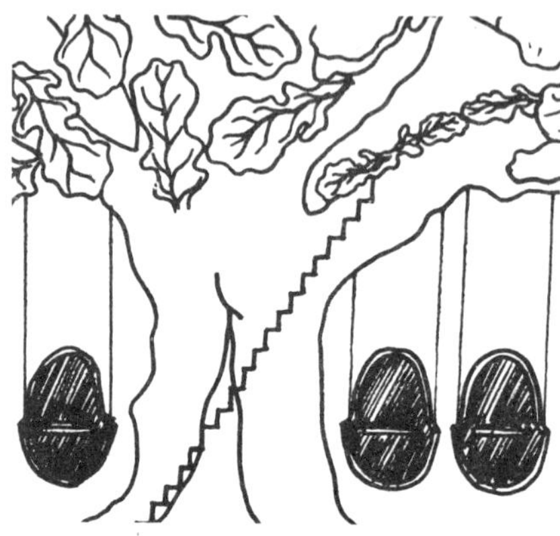

Garden of earthly delights II
Dorian Burt

A manipulation of available space designed to incorporate local resources and provide a fantasy land through which children can realise their dreams.

Born 1948 in Ilford, Essex. Studied sculpture at the Royal College of Art and was awarded a two-year scholarship to study in Japan. Lectures in ceramics at Carlisle College of Art.

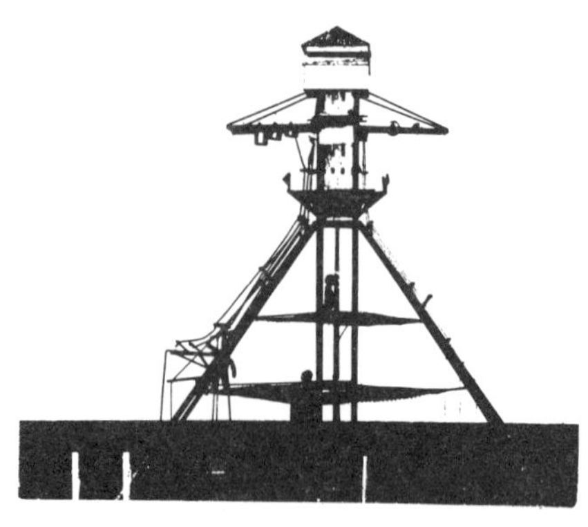

Musical pyramid
Paul Morris

Objectives: A pyramid forms a centrepiece in the play area. This visually exciting structure should be irresistible, challenging and exciting without being dangerous (children may climb to a great height in safety—the pyramid shape ensures that no one will fall far). Layout: The pyramid is enclosed along with several other features by an outer wall. The wall prevents entry except at 2 points top and bottom of the incline, where bridges are positioned. Children can then follow a series of walkways and ladders to the central feature, which also contains sound-making apparatus activated by the children from inside the tower. The sounds produced will be variable but muted (for the sake of the housing estate tenants). Materials: The structure will be made from simple, robust and easily available materials, i.e. telegraph poles, rope, wire mesh, reconstituted railway sleepers and specially designed metal cleats.

Born 1945. Studied at the Royal College of Art. Works as designer and lectures at Gwent College of Higher Education.

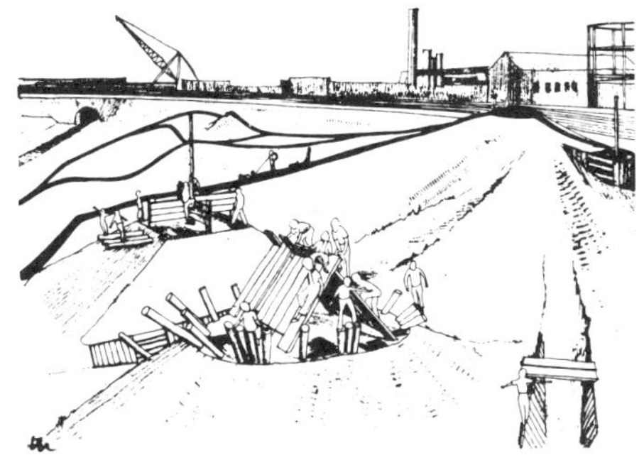

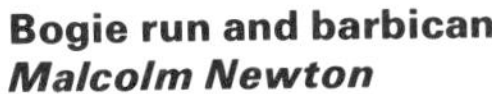

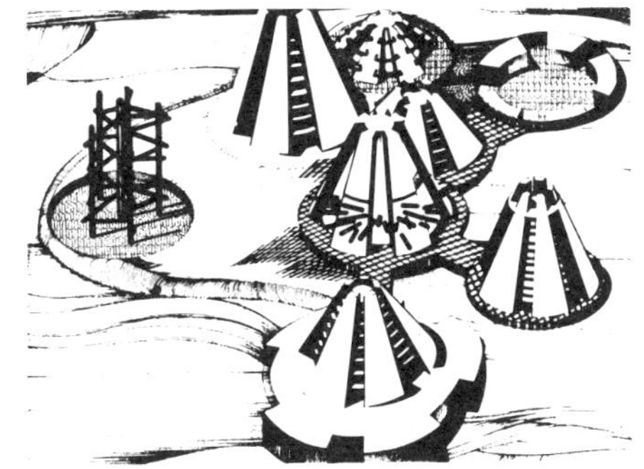

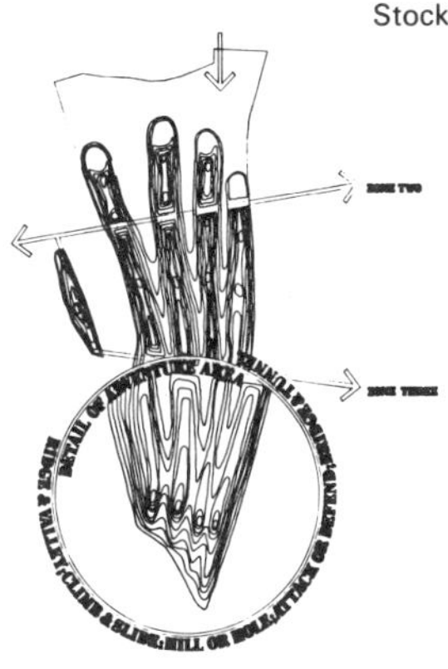

Bogie run and barbican
Malcolm Newton

The erstwhile dares and challenges of kids have generally been banned or organised into controlled, overseen activities. This site gives an opportunity to create landforms and structures adaptable to some of the many games needing varying degrees of skill and daring, unsupervised by adults. Spoil is used to form steep hills and valleys and the area covered with topsoil and seeded. These sharp contours form the framework. A bitmac track runs from the highest summit to the lowest point, giving several runs of differing difficulty for bogies, skateboards, bikes, etc. Steep gulches and ravines are formed within sleeper-retaining-walls and the tops of the hills have structures of sleepers and telegraph poles for further play. On part of the north-facing slope the gradient has been kept uniform for a long sledge run. Supervision is nil and maintenance minimal—at most two tractor mows per season.

Born 1942 in Skegness. Studied architecture and landscape design. Works as architect and market gardener.

Play cones
Deanna Petherbridge

The play cones are designed to take the place of conventional items of play equipment and would require little maintenance. Although based on the same pentaxial plan, the cones vary in height and diameter with either steps or metal bars ascending to the parapeted tops. As well as being objects for climbing on or sliding down (taller cones and those with projecting bars would be set into sand filled pits), they are large enough to suggest more imaginative play—as castles, or spaceships, etc. The bases of the play cones (plinths or pits) are partially excavated out of the hillside or built up in response to the slope of the site. The rest of the Durham Road site is landscaped, using the same plan unit as the play cones of the play area. Paths, plinths and areas are paved in brick and the play cones are constructed out of granite paviors, or could use railway-sleepers as permanent shuttering.

Born 1939 in Pretoria. Studied fine art. Works as painter, researcher and writer and teaches art history.

A helping hand
Simon Smithson

The hand placed on the site has fingers as ridges running lengthways. The fingertips, not quite touching the Durham Road boundary of the site, leave flat tracts of land between the ridges for more formal games. Play equipment for the bairns and seating for parents are on the plateau of the finger-nails; the main pedestrian route cuts across the fingers at the joints. Between the joints and the knuckles the fingerbone-like mounds form higher ridges, which come closer and closer together. The thumb rests on a small island of land between railway lines; along it runs a path linking the pedestrian route, which crosses the site at the joints, to the secondary route which crosses at the knuckles. Below the knuckles the ridges are yet closer together and the valleys between the ridges deeper, culminating in peaks just above the wrist. This is the adventure area. The nature of the terrain suggests the game, either on foot or on bike.

Born 1954 in London. Works in architect's office.

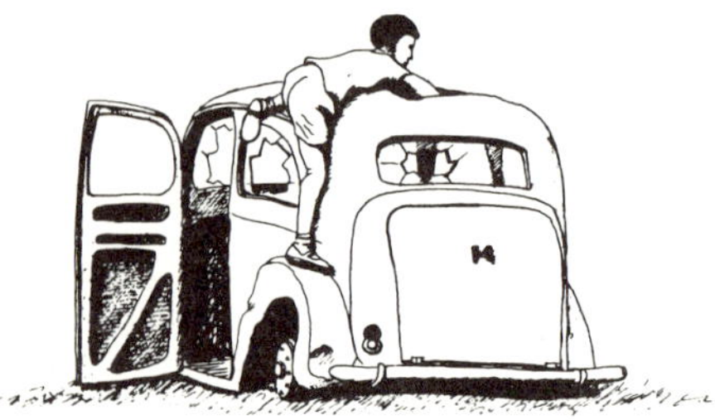

Vandal Park
John Spargo

The Vandal Park is designed to exhaust the vandalistic instincts of the local children. It does this by providing them with an area ideal for gang warfare and other vandal-like activities such as painting graffiti on walls, wrecking cars, breaking windows, etc. The park also provides them with the ultimate challenge to remove a £5 note from between two sheets of unbreakable armour-plated glass. Initial attraction to the park is provided by the areas being fenced off and by the Council's notices forbidding entry.

Born 1953 in London. Studies interior design at Middlesex Polytechnic.

Look-out over Kingsbury Water Park

Provide extensive views over lakes reclaimed for leisure

The site is located in the Kingsbury Water Park which the Warwickshire County Council is creating at Bodymoor Heath near Sutton Coldfield. The park is based on a series of worked out and partially restored wet gravel workings in the valley of the River Tame. It was opened to the public in 1975 and will continue to be developed over the period until 1982.

At present the park consists of about 100 hectares of land and water and provides a wide variety of both water and land based recreational activities. The park has proved very popular and draws visitors from a wide area of the Midlands. Visitors can wander along the lakesides or explore the footpaths and trails. They can picnic on the beaches, or drive into the main picnic area. The energetic can play ball games on the grassed areas or fly kites and there is an adventure playground for the young. The less active can relax by the lakeside and watch others fishing, hydroplaning or sailing. For enthusiasts the public fishing facilities are good, the area abounds in unusual wildlife and the Tamworth Sailing Club and Midlands Hydroplane Club provide facilities for members to enjoy these exciting sports. A display centre has been provided explaining what to look for in the Water Park so that visitors can derive more enjoyment from their visit.

The site for the project is adjacent to the main car park and to the recently constructed public activity pools in the centre of the park. The County Council is looking for a feature with a vertical emphasis which will visually identify the focal point of the park and will also provide viewing facilities for visitors.

Brief

The design should:

1. Provide a feature with a vertical emphasis which will form a visual focal point in the flat landscape of the park.
2. Provide views over the park.
3. Be constructed of elm which has been felled locally as a result of Dutch Elm Disease, or of other natural material in sympathy with the surrounding landscape.
4. Be accessible, if possible, to all age groups.
5. Be permanent, robust, fire resistent and with a low maintenance requirement.

The design may:

1. Incorporate static water by excavating the ground to below the water table.

The design must not:

1. Interfere with the public footpath which crosses the site.
2. Disturb the existing areas of the water.

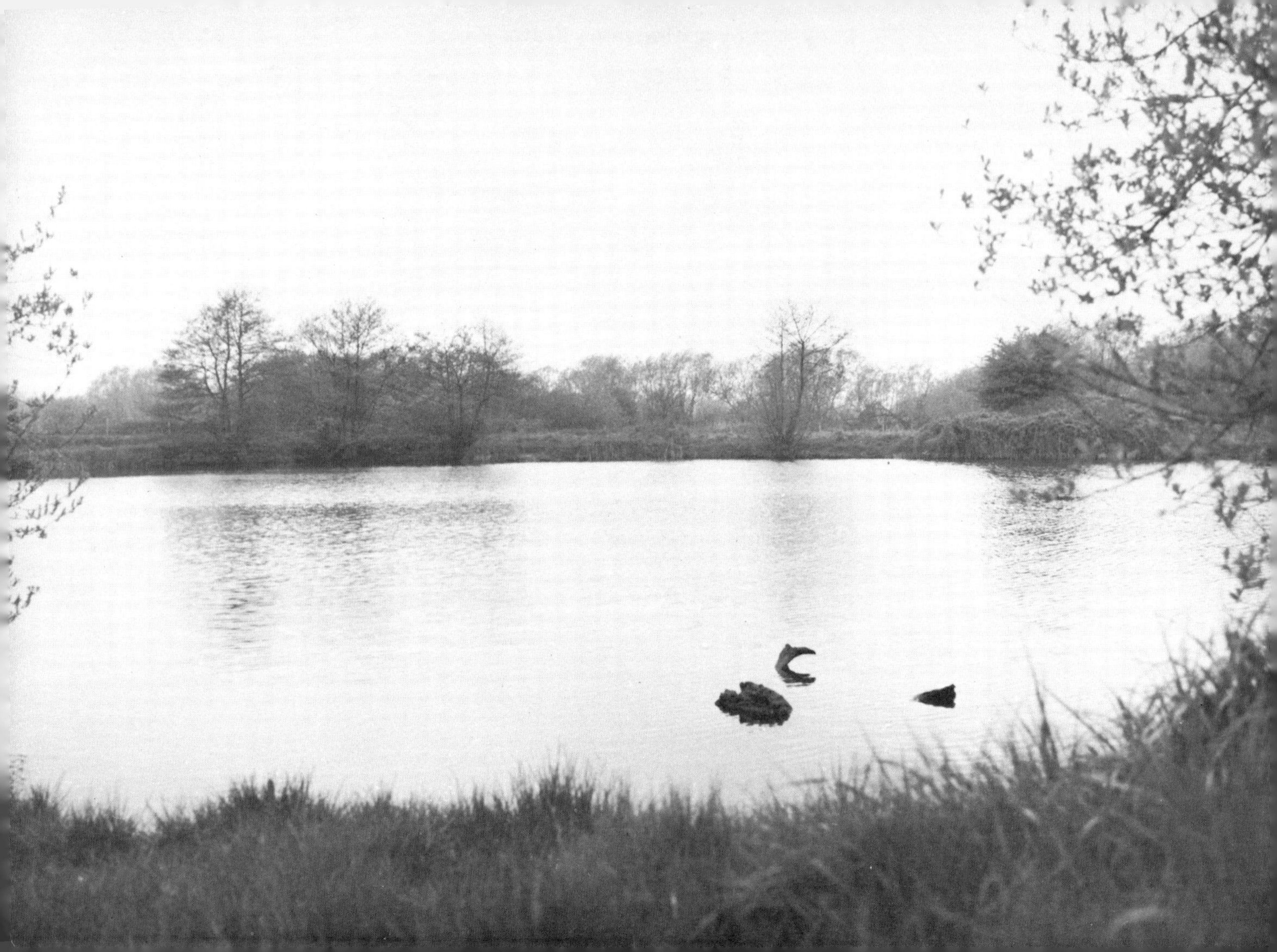

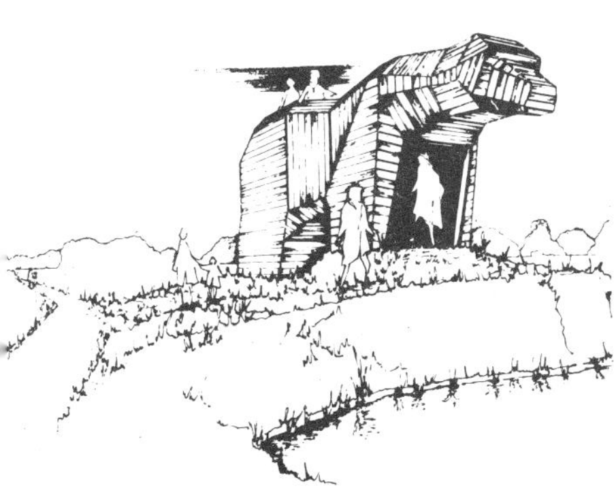

Bear look-out
Julian Brafman

The nature of the construction makes a natural focal point within the area; its individuality will automatically attract people to it. The hollow statue will enable people to mount to a high platform from where they will have a commanding view of the landscape. The bears are to be constructed of Dutch Elm-diseased-timber. The look-out is designed to be maintenance-free and the timber, having been weather- and fire-proofed, will remain in that natural state of finish. The mound upon which the larger bear stands will be created with earth dug from a newly made pond which is positioned beneath the bear's head so as to create the illusion that the bear is looking out over water. Finally, the bear is intended to reflect the Warwickshire Coat-of-Arms and also serve as an emblem for the water park.

Born 1953 in London. Studies interior design at Middlesex Polytechnic.

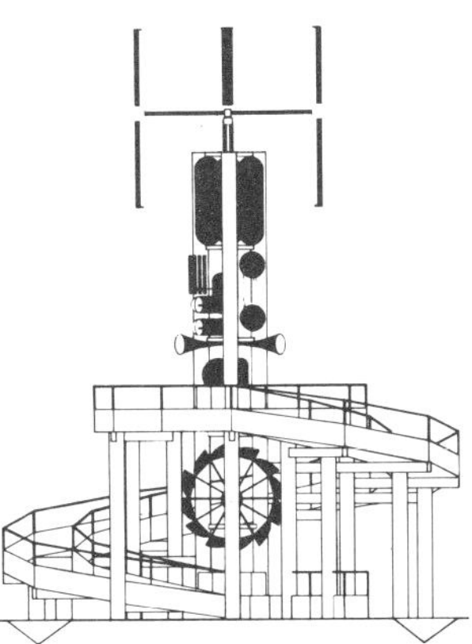

Ambient energy tower
John Csáky, Simon Conolly

The 10m high timber tower supports a number of ambient energy converters and storage devices, the behaviour of which will respond to changes in the weather. They will give an opportunity for comparative evaluation of their strengths and demonstrate their potential usefulness. The equipment will be labelled to show its purpose and capacity. A vertical axis windmill pumps water from the pool surrounding the base of the tower up to the storage tanks. A proportion of this water is released to pour over a water wheel. A solar collector warms and circulates the water. Sounds will come from a number of audio instruments such as solar trumpets, humming mirror blades, bells, a wind and water harp, and a solar system organ.

John Csáky born 1945 in Shrewsbury. Studied at Portsmouth College of Art and Royal College of Art. Currently designing a large earth concert bowl.

Simon Conolly born 1946 in Dublin. Studied at the Architectural Association. Specializes in lightweight structures.

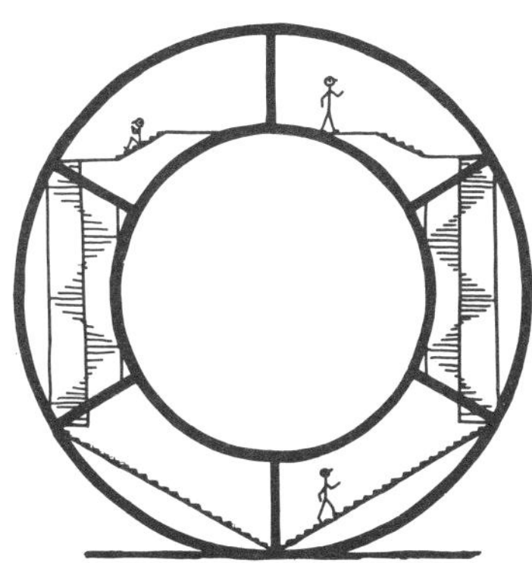

Wonder wheel
Peter Finnimore

A large wooden wheel 13.5m in diameter. Steps and spiral staircases give access to the lookout platform. The height is just enough to allow a view over neighbouring treetops. The wheel can also shelter people from wind and rain and would look sufficiently interesting from a distance to invite closer investigation but not so bizarre that it would clash with the rural setting.

Born 1944. Works as technician at the Open University.

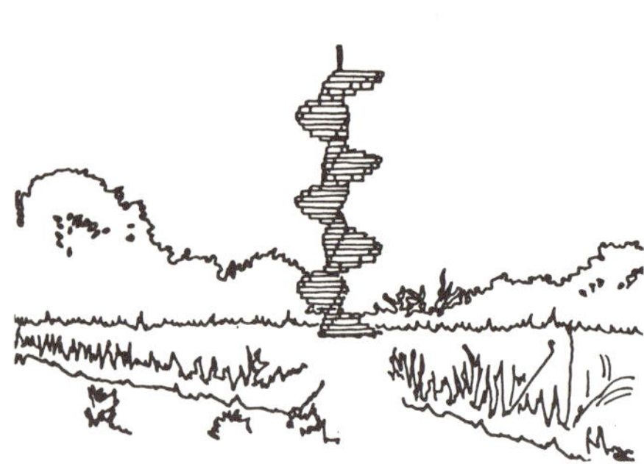

Spiral
David Foster

The design provides a feature with vertical emphasis to form a visual focal point in the flat landscape of the park. It can be climbed to provide views over the park. It is constructed of solid or laminated slabs of locally felled elm, arranged spirally about a concrete-filled steel column. It is permanent, robust, fire resistant and requires minimal maintenance. It might for further effect be sited atop an artificial earth mound.

Born 1953 in London. Studies at the Architectural Association.

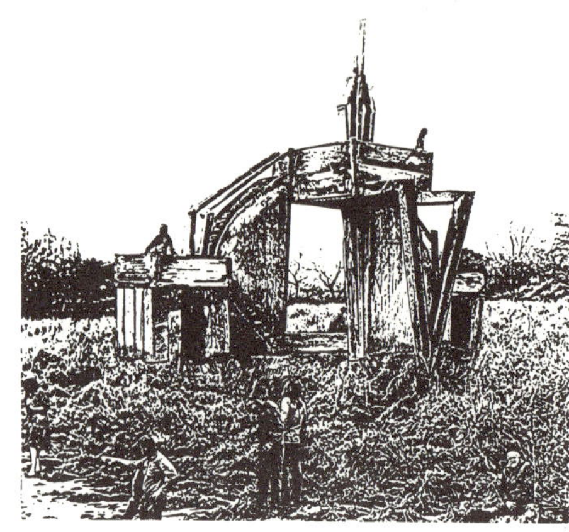

Elm construction
Virginia Gordon

Until recently Kingsbury village, which stands on a hill overlooking the water park, was a quiet backwater (the setting for George Eliot's *Mill on the Floss*). Now it is divided by the A51 from Birmingham, and little of its original atmosphere remains. The inhabitants are divided in their attitudes to the park—the older nostalgic for the past, the summer evenings spent fishing and swimming, the freedom to explore; the younger inhabitants appreciating the newly organized recreational facilities. The village retains two distinctive features, the water mill and the church, whose spire dominates the hill. My proposal aims to reflect these elements, the spirit of the place and its inhabitants. Made of local elm, it would be both monumental and strongly related to its surroundings. There are three lookout platforms; ascent and descent is by stairs or by flights of wedgeshaped risers and baulks of timber (the latter serving as seats and stairs). The spire rises to 40ft.

Born 1937 in Hove. Studied at RADA. Works as mother and is interested in sculpture.

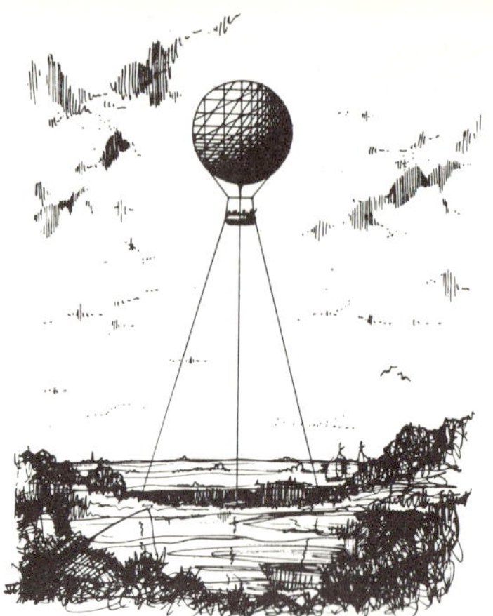

Aerostat
Trevor Grant

Floating high over the park on gossamer threads the crimson sphere beckons. Walking by lakes, through woodland, along paths, glimpsing this landmark expectations rise. Mounting the triangular plinth, paying the attendant, you enter and sit beside your fellow 'travellers' around the circumference of the circular nacelle. Firstly the wickerwork creaks then, save the breeze in the rigging, silently the ground slowly falls away. Pausing at about 60 m you sway gently, seemingly suspended by the finest guy wires from the giant red 10 m diameter helium balloon 'Aerostat' above your heads. Far below the taut steel tethering cables stretch back to the winch-dias; people scurry ant-like, toy boats skim over looking-glass lakes and roads and fields recede far into the distance to the towns encircling the horizon. There you must return, but now you hover peacefully over the diminished world below, silently summoning others like you!

Born 1951 in Mowsley, Leicestershire. Studies at Newcastle University School of Architecture.

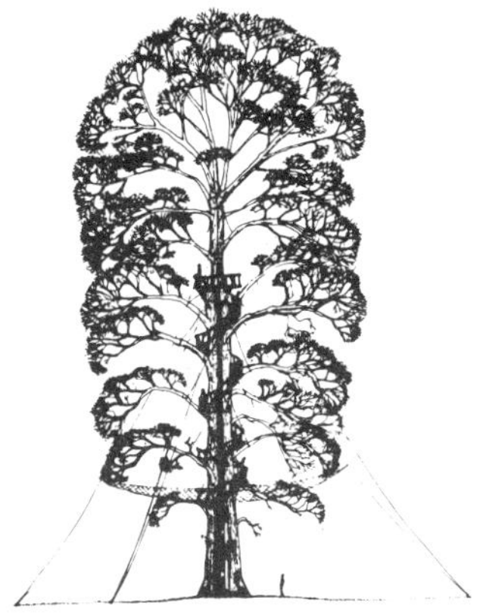

Monument to the fallen elm
David Halford

The elm needs some kind of memorial: this scheme provides the equivalent of a statue of the unknown soldier. The structure takes the form of a giant elm tree, fabricated from felled elms and given rigidity by telegraph poles and steel cables. Its height provides the vertical feature called for in the brief and there is access, by rustic spiral stairs, to a look-out platform. The proposal is intended to maintain a harmony with the surrounding landscape while being sufficiently artificial to act as a 'feature'.

Born 1953 in Peterborough. Studied at Thames Polytechnic. Now studies architecture at University College School of Environmental Studies.

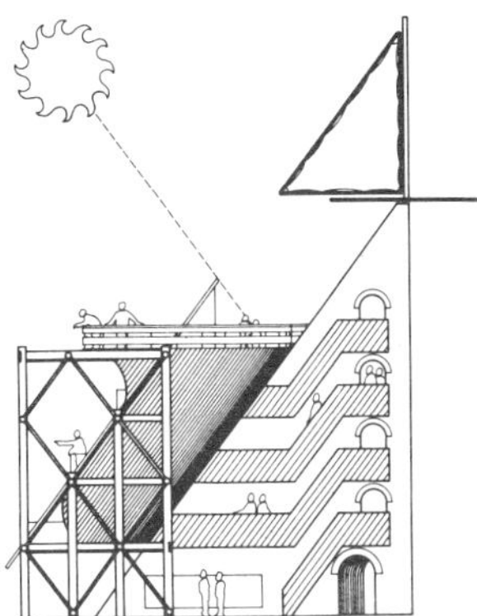

Sun and wind
Joe Holyoak

I used to visit Kingsbury as a bicycling adolescent and remember the elemental nature of the flooded gravel workings—confirmed by more recent visits. The flat landscape is open to the sun and sky, and the wind continually sweeps up the exposed river valley. The tower responds by performing the functions of a wind vane and a sundial, and is composed of suitably elemental forms. There are four dials which give the correct solar time at the summer and winter equinoxes and the spring and autumn solstices. The dials are shaped so as to represent the extent of the sun's passage through 262 degrees between sunrise and sunset at the summer equinox, through 180 degrees at the two solstices, and through 98 degrees at the winter equinox. The visitor ascends from sundial to sundial through a series of staircases topped by a large red triangular vane, visible from a long distance.

Born 1944 in Birmingham. Studied at Birmingham School of Architecture. Works as architect and planning consultant.

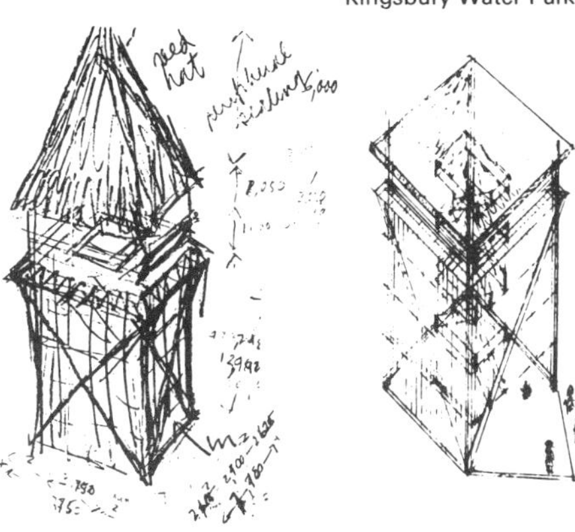

5-layered look-out
A M Smithson

Built of Warwickshire elm and stained with brightly coloured wood preservative, the five structures allow people to view the surrounding terrain from five levels. A moving view at ground level, The Swing Look-out: a reed thatched pavilion sturdy enough to take adults swinging on a knotted ship's rope. One easy ramp above ground makes Marsh Platform Look-out accessible to disabled people, cyclists, children in pushchairs; the parapet would be engraved with compass directions and the names of visible local features. Two flights above the ground Straight Climb Look-out: a smaller platform under an open-frame roof. Three flights: Flag Tower Platform, a larger platform through which the central cage containing a rung ladder allows both another way up from the ground and access to a crows-nest into which children and young people can climb. Four flights: Heron's View Look-out, where a reed-thatched roof shelters the platform.

Born 1928 in Sheffield. Works as architect in private practice.

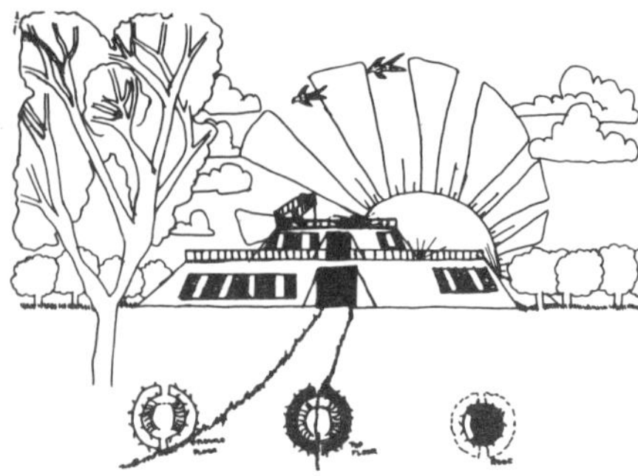

Look-around Kingsbury
Soraya Smithson

The look-around has two floors for one reason: to allow bird watchers to watch birds feeding or flying. There are windows nearly all the way round but mostly facing out to the fishing pool and the marshy area; they have no glass and are in their own individual boxes and have shutters that slide along. The shutters are mainly there to stop the glare from the fishing pool and the marshy area. The Look-around is entirely round and looks like a flying saucer. It is made of wood because of all the spare elm wood around Warwickshire and also to make it fit slightly in with its surroundings. The stairs go all the way up inside the drum. The stairs that lead out onto the roof come up inside a little hut which has a sloping roof with a railing around it because children will run up and down it like I did in the Corb house in Paris. Also, the terrace and roof have rails around them.

Born 1964 in London. Attends Pimlico Comprehensive School.

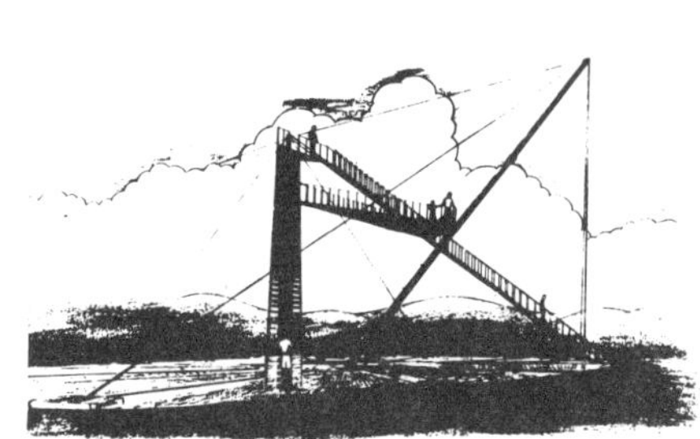

Sundial look-out
John Spargo

The Sundial look-out is constructed of felled elm and is held in position by steel cables. The three large lengths of timber used in the structure are formed by laminating large beams of elm, the joints being glued and bolted. Two staircases, one up and one down, provide access to the two look-out platforms at $24\frac{1}{4}$ft and $35\frac{1}{2}$ft above ground level. The sundial face is covered with cobblestones, the hours being marked by stainless steel numerals mounted on concrete frames. The hours are also marked by troughs of water which radiate out to the numerals from a central pond so that the shadow cast on the dial face blots out the reflections on the water at each hour.

Born 1953 in London. Studies interior design at Middlesex Polytechnic.

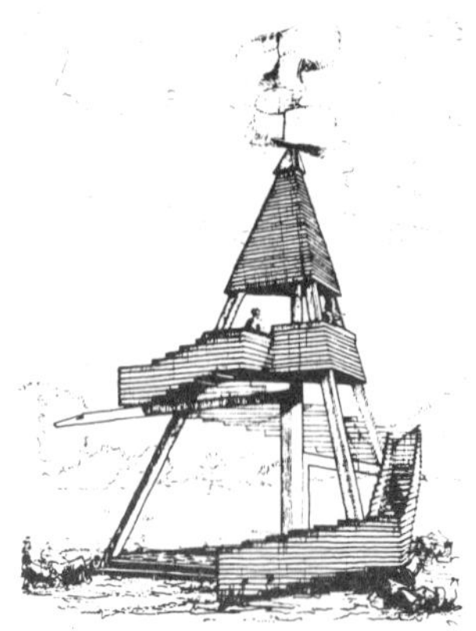

Trickle splash gush
Anthony Vogt, Neil Morrison, Adrian Lock

To create movement and delight in the static charm of the existing park, the solid elm pyramidal structure is used as the basis of a viewing tower and supports the wind actuated rotor, which by a simple pump raises water from marsh land to serve a set of water shoots. The result will be a constantly changing 'live' tower with the colour mixture rotor varying in revolution speed with the wind, and actuating the different shoots from a slow minimal trickle in light winds to a full gush in strong winds.

Anthony Vogt born 1932 in London. Studied architecture at University College London. Lectures at the Mackintosh School of Architecture, Glasgow.

Neil Morrison born 1944 in Aberdeen. Works as painter and lute builder and lectures at Glasgow School of Art.

Adrian Lock born 1935 in Devizes. Works as naval architect.

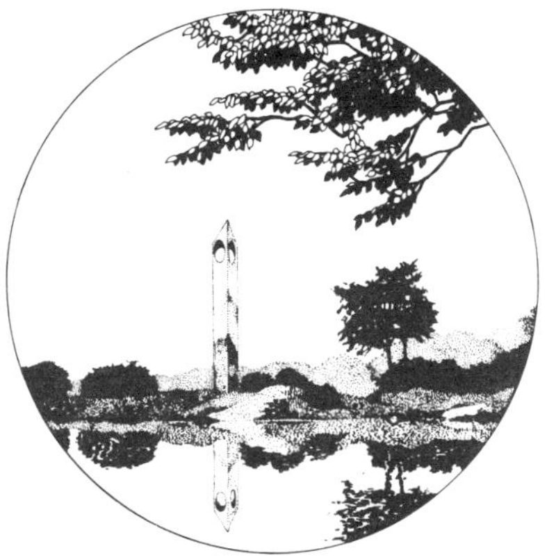

Stuff the genius loci?
Derek Walker Associates

The design solution is a look-out, look-in tower. A simple, tubular-steel-framed, mirror-clad, triangular column, with minimal detailing on the outer skin. Climb it and look out over the water park. Pass it by and look in at the reflections of the trees, grass, water and people. A glass column on a raised circular grassy plinth, surrounded by a still, reflective moat, set in a field of uncut grass and from a distance an intriguing needle of glass reflecting sunlight and sky.
Architectural practice.

Arts Council of Great Britain 1977
Exhibition organised by Sue Grayson
with practical advice from David Rock
and assistance from Peggy Armstrong and Joanna
Hordern
Catalogue designed by Emanuel Sandreuter
Cover image by Patrick Hughes
Printed by Hill+Garwood Printing Limited